ROCKSTARS AND EXECUTIONS

Andrew Mallin

Rockstars and Executions
by Andrew Mallin

Copyright © 2022 by Andrew Mallin

All rights reserved. No part of this book may be reproduced or used in any manner without written permission of the copyright owner except for the use of quotations in a book review. For more information, address: author.andrew.mallin@gmail.com

First paperback edition October 2022

Cover design by Brian C. Mallin
Edited by David Twiddy

ISBN 979-8-9870011-0-3 (paperback)
ISBN 979-8-9870011-1-0 (ebook)

www.andrewmallin.com

Dedication

*For those who have fallen,
You'll Never Walk Alone*

TABLE OF CONTENTS

Dedication v

Prelude ix

Introduction xi

Day One: Kathleen Behan 13

                  Frank Sumner 15

Day Two: Kathleen 25

                  Frank 26

Day Three: Kathleen 39

                  Frank 41

Day Four: Kathleen 57

                  Frank 63

Day Five: Kathleen 79

                  Frank 81

Day Six: Kathleen 99

                  Frank 102

Day Seven: Kathleen 119

                  Interlude 121

	Frank	123
Day Eight:	Kathleen	129
	Frank	130
Day Nine:	Kathleen	137
	Frank	137
Day Ten:	Kathleen	147
	Frank	148
Day Eleven:	Kathleen	163
	Frank	167
Day Twelve:	Kathleen	179
	Frank	181
Day Thirteen:	Kathleen	193
	Frank	198
Day Fourteen:	Kathleen	217
	Frank	227
About the Author		259

Prelude

Angola, the site of the Louisiana State Penitentiary. Water on three sides, churches on the other. The heat rises in waves from the ground, and the stink of the plantation is rich. Men work the fields outside, or they wait to die in tiers inside. The Mississippi River and swamps on three sides, churches on the other, and all the men inside killing themselves might not be suicides.

From a Philadelphia jail, a young man writes to her as he waits to die, accused of killing an off-duty cop, guilty of being in the area when the cops responded. A barrage of evidence proving his innocence was ignored by the state's prosecutor, working with a pair of evidence-fixing detectives. Who cared? Nobody cared. He told me Kathleen walked in as if on angel's wings.

That's Kathleen Behan — "Kitty" to her friends. Then my memories shift to those of Frank—the yogi, Mister Loco to his friends from Miami. He takes the beeper out of his pocket and, excusing himself to Billy Joel, heads to a hotel room down the hall to call his associate on the shrimping boat. He's in a tight black shirt, sunglasses on at all times, and his job is to just about rip the arms off anyone who tries to get too near Billy Joel.

The security gig is a favor for old friends, a reunion of comrades from many rock and roll shows, and a distraction from his cocaine empire. He likes Billy, though; he likes the buzz of the big shows and being part of a machine, and the people around rock stars hoover up his cocaine. He had stood out at the cockfights in Miami, a gringo in a crowd of Cubans and Colombians, and he had to prove himself to the Cubans despite being vouched for by the Gonzalez brothers. The Gonzalez brothers, who cornered the DHL freight connection where the cocaine went in and out the back gate at Miami airport. The Gonzalez brothers said he was good, he proved himself, and like that he went from being in the marijuana business to being the largest cocaine dealer in the mid-Atlantic, delivering packages from Boston to Miami and Virginia Beach to Nashville. Business was great, but Billy Joel was a lot of fun to be around. Billy Joel was nothing like the fussy Prince, who'd made an ass out of himself in front of Chuck Norris.

I woke up. The interviews had taken over my life.

Introduction

Here's how it goes: when Frank needs a memory jog, he will call a friend. He always has his phone close to hand, and intermittently as we talk, mid-sentence I'll hear it start ringing on the other end. The other person answers and greets Frank warmly. Frank wastes little time. "Hey, [legal name], I need your help remembering something. Now, when we were in [place] and we were [committing major crimes] and there was that [more major crimes we did together], do you remember who was driving? By the way, I'm with the story man, Andrew, and he's writing all this down." Well, the person on the other end of the line will occasionally cut Frank off with some form of, "Wait, what the fuck? Who is listening to this? I don't know what you're talking about. Now, who the fuck is on the line with you Hammer, and why?" Or, and this is by far the most common outcome, they'll launch right into a wildly incriminating answer: "Yeah, it was me." or "Oh man, that was so long ago. Was that the fat guy's buddy, who we did Billy Joel with?"

My older brother is one of these surfing nutjobs who go down to the beach at ungodly o'clock in the morning to gauge the waves. It's a small, energetic, and friendly community. Some days an older guy who goes by Yogi or Frank can be found at the beach at the same psychotically early hours. Frank will be there doing breathing exercises, looking at the stars, or doing some other spiritual stuff. Prod him and Frank tells strangers stories about moving weight, about being a gangster, about hanging out with Elvis and walking Jimi Hendrix on stage, touring with Prince and The Beach Boys. I had just finished my first fiction book, I'd months ago quit my latest and last job as a Geographer, and I was hiding from my impending financial doom. I wasn't sure what to expect, other than that I'd hear some rock and roll stories, and *Almost Famous* is a terrific movie, so why not live this bit of the dream while I'm going broke? That is how I ended up knocking on the door of Frank Sumner and Kathleen Behan ten years to the day after my final drink.

    I knock and Frank Sumner answers the door. "Christopher?" It's Andrew. We've met in person twice before and talked on the phone to coordinate this interview. He closed the door behind me grinning, and when he smiles it's like seeing a shark swimming your way in water that's just a bit too deep. "Close enough." We are off to a flyer.

Day One, 2/14/22

Kathleen Behan

I didn't know I'd be meeting with Kathleen Behan. Frank had not mentioned her once as we discussed and planned these interviews, but now she shuffles into the room where we'll be doing these interviews. Her face is intelligent, wild, and twisted by the strokes. Kathleen A. Behan of Stone Mountain, Georgia, who went four days without eating as a child and remembered that hunger every day she was at Yale and then Columbia Law School.

Being tone deaf, my first question for her is about Frank.

"He's a spiritual person and a yogi, a yoga expert. He gives me advice throughout the day, he walks me, he motivates me—and believe me, he is motivational. I would not be walking if it wasn't for him."

What followed was a stream of milestones in her life, accomplishments that I could not keep pace with, and only later did I wonder why I barely tried to keep pace. I was happy to pretend to write what she was saying down. At least at first.

Kathleen had helped get her first innocent guy off death row while she was still a student. She played a part in the founding of the Tahirih Justice Center after a friend had met a woman who had suffered female genital mutilation and they set out to help other women in similarly bad situations. She had started international women's reading groups. She was named a top forty under-forty attorney in America. She made partner at Arnold & Porter in Washington, D.C., agreeing to the promotion only after striking a deal to continue taking on an aggressive amount of pro-bono work. She is an alcoholic and drank heavily throughout her successful career. Kathleen has survived four strokes. The first three ended her legal career, the fourth put her in a coma.

"I was born in Milwaukee, Wisconsin, one of six kids. My dad had a small art supply store in town, and I was six years old when he lost the store. The family drove to Arizona on the promise of a job for dad selling cars, but things went from bad to worse and hunger became a feature of life. The whole family was sleeping in the station wagon. I went four days without eating at one point.

"Finally, my mother found work teaching home economics at a community college in Georgia, and with mom vouching for him, my father found work at the school. I grew up in Stone Mountain, Georgia. The Klan was there, and the racism was terrible. I didn't have a dollar to my name, but I made certain I had a four-point-oh (grade point average).

"An ex-Clinton lawyer came to the firm and said that they needed help, so I flew to Zurich and met my new client. Marc Rich was a Holocaust baby. He grew up and got a job in the mailroom at one of the big trading companies. He worked his way from the mailroom to being the very top trader at his company. Then he said, "Hey guys, I want to take this overseas because we have the 'no trading with enemies acts,' and we can go right around (them) if we take the business abroad." So, he goes overseas and sets up a shop where he can trade oil with America's paper enemies. Marc met a guy, Pincus Green; he was the face, Marc the brains. Switzerland was making tons in taxes off the trading these two guys were doing, and all of this pissed off USA tax authorities. Rudy Giuliani called to offer to drop all legal harassment if Marc Rich and Pincus would move their company home to the United States. Marc Rich and Pincus Green were of the opinion that Giuliani could get fucked. It would've been cheaper to deal with Rudy, but in the end, Marc Rich settled with the federal government, paying six hundred million dollars voluntarily to be able to return home."

Kathleen says nice to meet you, gives me a fist bump, and is gone. I'm not entirely sure what just happened.

*****

Frank Sumner

He's not even through the door before he starts.

"I had to think all the time. I had to keep my close friends close because they were the only people I could trust to work with. There are two things you got to do if you're going to work with me. The first is have a history of being straight with me. The second is you don't go to any attorney except my attorney. If you go to see any other attorney than mine you have to face punishment.

"You need to have a good bondsman. He needs to be able to go up to a million in a flash. I remember one time I was getting out on bond. The judge sets the bond, but the payment or whatever is set up by this woman who's like a clerk in some other part of the courthouse. And I'm standing there unrepentant, and I got a certain 'fuck you' attitude, so I was kinda messing with her while she was processing me, making fun of the whole thing. She looked at me real serious and says, 'I hate people like you.' Well, right then a couple police officers walk by, and some of them ask me if I want anything from the sandwich shop, friendly as can be. I could see she knew they worked for me. But what did I care? I got out of there. They had found four kilos in one of my cars, and I was only in custody for four hours.

"My family is part Irish, part Greek, part Italian. My father was fourteen and his oldest brother, Stanley, was sixteen when their father killed their mother. It was 1934, the Depression, and I guess things weren't going well. So, my grandfather took a shotgun and blew his wife's head off. Then he took a shot at one of my dad's younger brothers; he got away just barely by running around the corner of the house. My grandpa then kinda realized what he'd done, and he reloaded that shotgun and took his own head off.

"My uncle Stanley got married later that same year. He was sixteen, and he was a gangster. He took care of people; he tried to help. He started taking care of his family, and he got his brothers into the trucking business. That meant trucking produce around, supplying different markets in the cities, but it also meant moving cigarettes and booze. Trips to Boston, New York, then back to Portsmouth, Virginia. Stanley and Dad served in World War II

"I think because of who was in my family I picked it up soon, but I think I would've been in the business one way or another. Uncle Stanley would call me Little Frankie, and he took me everywhere. He would always get a kick out of parking in the No Parking spots where the signs were, doing it in front of cops, laughing because they wouldn't do shit to him. He would treat me to breakfast and take me to get ice cream.

— **Andrew Mallin** —

"Stanley told me a story when I was still pretty young: he would hire the police as help when he was delivering shit in his truck; a cop would follow on some deliveries. So, he tells me about this time he's dropping shit off, only the money wasn't right. So he had a bit of an argument, went outside, rapped on the door, asked the cop to come back in five minutes. The cop says sure. Stanley went inside and shot one of the guys in the leg. The cop comes back five minutes later and says, "Come on man, you didn't just shoot somebody, did ya?" because he could see the guy and the blood, and Stanley told that cop he didn't see anything, but he'd let him know real quick if he saw anyone suspect-looking. Uncle Stanley taught me a lot.

"Stanley got in a bit of trouble and died in a high-speed car chase with the cops and (was) going about a hundred and twenty miles per hour when his car went off the highway there in Norfolk, Virginia. That was before (I went to) high school. I had a punching bag and was getting into it at my mother and father's house. I was in a Catholic school; upper middle class, so I went to Catholic school and that's where I learned how rich kids are. I learned about how the way the mind works in a person like that. I learned a lot from Stanley and from the way a lot of people think they deserve something.

"I'd be at my parents' house, and I would watch the bus for the Navy Yard go by every day. I wanted to do anything except do the same thing every day. I kept working on my boxing and got into the martial arts. We would go to Beacons pool hall on High Street—that's where I met the guy who hired me at the Navy Yard. The Navy Yard is there. You've got Marines and Army too. We'd leave school, play pool, and work out, and I was buff, brother. I was big, fast, and I could fight. I could just go.

"I was playing pool at Beacons when I got the ship yard job. The guy who gave me the job says there are two guys in a motorcycle gang who are giving him a tough time, says 'I need you to look after them, and I'll give you the job.' And I said, 'sure,' and I beat the shit out of those two guys. First day on the job, well, that's what I had to do.

"One of the guys I beat up became my closest friend. He was with a bike gang, the Renegades, and they were a shit outfit—they were all over the place, they weren't doing shit right. So, the guy who I had just beat the shit out of says, 'Hey man, you want to help selling this weed?' and that's how we became friends. They had pounds of weed they would drop in bales near Elizabeth City, outside Norfolk. I was into it, I liked the business. Then this same buddy says there's a credit union that we can take down real easy. I said no to that, I wanted to be a businessman.

"So, I'm working at the shipyard and we're learning how to weld shit, how to break shit down, and so we start doing some more stupid criminal shit. Everyone knows me at the yard by this point, right? I've been around a while, I'm just another body, so we started stealing lead from the yard. We were already stealing copper pipe. Prices of copper, brass, and lead were way, way up because of the Vietnam War. So, we stole that shit, me and my friends.

"Jerry Bass was part Cherokee. He was the biggest racist I ever met. His brother was a KKK dragon, and Jerry went to school with me. Jerry is doing some work with the Union of Steel Workers and Jerry asks me to beat up the head of the union. Jerry—I used to call 'Choo-choo' because he would always wear these bib overalls like a train conductor—and Jerry is this big, fat, mean, racist son of a bitch, and Jerry says if you beat the shit out of this guy then (he) will be head of the union. Jerry came back to me a week later and says we can't just beat this guy up, we gotta kill him. I did not get on alright with Jerry, and I thought Jerry did not know what he was doing; plus, I had a one-year-old kid, and I figured if I killed someone for Jerry I'd have to kill Jerry too. Jerry goes to do it solo and gets caught! I was sitting there home at night, watching the TV with my one-year-old kid, and there's Jerry like a week after our talk, getting walked in cuffs in front of a shitload of cameras—attempted murder. Trouble, that's what we called Jerry. He had him a perm. What an idiot.

"It was around that time I decided to go big. I had met some marijuana people, I had some longshoremen as friends, and I went from ounces to pounds to pallets. I went to guys in each shop—woodworking, ironworking shop, the guys in control of every shop—and I introduced myself as a guy in the marijuana business. I went to the chrome shop, then the garbage guys. Then all the guys who worked the cranes, the gantries, and the big hammerhead cranes, all of them. It didn't take a rocket scientist to go big. Then sometime in the mid '70s there was some budget cuts or some DoD (Department of Defense) changes, big changes. My boss, Toller, came to me and says, 'Frank, I got to let you go, I got no choice.' I told him I don't care if he demotes me to stacking pencils, I need to be in the shipyard, I got too much business to do there. Toller just says 'sorry man.'

"I waited outside Toller's house that night. I showed him the gun, asked him how he was doing? Asked him if he was thinking of rethinking? The next day in the office Toller made a little speech to the other guys in our shop and gave me a promotion.

"I got better and better at running stuff through the shipyard. At the same time, I was starting to do the shows. Jimi Hendrix came to Virginia Beach and maybe five hundred people showed up. That was my first time working security and walking the band on stage. The next year, Hendrix came back and you couldn't even move on the streets there were so many fucking people trying to get into the venue.

"I wanted to keep growing things at the shipyard. I didn't think much of the rock and roll security gig at first. I needed a place to keep shit, so I bought a big apartment in a complex that abutted the ship yard—that's where I stashed my first couple cars and I would store hundreds of pounds of marijuana. The shit came in bales. You gotta understand, the guys who work on the ground in the shipyard all carry tool bags and tool cases, and so it was nothing to stick a couple pounds of weed in a bag at work.

"Frank Coppola (name changed) died in the Virginia electric chair. He maintained his innocence until the day he died. I know he killed at least two people. He was a police officer who robbed Black folks and who was known to go in with people on robberies of jewelry stores. On my mother's side, she was Polish, maybe Hungarian too, and she had a big family. Her sister, my aunt, opened a grocery store in what was then called the 'darktown' in Norfolk. This was a meat market and grocer that my uncle Stanley and father and them would supply. So, I'd heard about the guy from some family who knew how he was, and I was selling some shit to Frank Coppola, pills and stuff. He got too fucking reckless, he got violent, and he got caught, and he pretty much fucked everything I had going at the shipyard in one go. He finally died in the chair in 1982."

Mike Agnar picks up on the second ring when Frank calls.

Mike: "What's up man? It's cold down here!"

Frank: "Mike, we just watched that video of you and Mike Wallace!"

Mike: "Ain't that something?"

Frank: "So did you do more than one *60 Minutes*?"

Mike: "Well, it took a couple hours to record the segments if I recall, but it was one story."

Frank: "Mike, you know I'm a trustworthy guy, right? That I'm straight, that you know I don't fuck around?"

Mike: "Yes."

Frank: "Well good, cause I'm here with a guy who wants to write the story up, and I was telling him about all the things we would do outside the drug business, the motorcycles and chasing women."

Mike: "You know it."

Frank: "I told him it was your father who leaned in real close one day and told me, he says 'All the bushes and all the trees have ears, all the bushes and the trees have ears.' You remember that? He knew the heat was on the shipyard."

Mike: "Yes."

Frank: "Hey, so we just watched you on *60 Minutes*, and it brought to mind hanging with Earl the Pearl. Do you remember that Earl story? I don't really remember where Villar's place was."

We had just watched the *60 Minutes* segment about Louis Villar's compounds in Coronado and on Hilton Head Island through which the Thai sticks of marijuana had been moved by the ton from 1972 to 1981. Then they got sloppy, and Mike Wallace was there some time after the wake.

Mike: "We met Earl the Pearl at a tennis clinic of all places. Earl was on Hilton Head and something got busted with his limousine, and we said, 'Shit man, come over if you want. We got a pool, we got a lot of women, we had the whole place to ourselves.' Villar was already . . . you know. So yeah, Earl came over and we hosted him for a night maybe. There was a basketball hoop near the carriage house, and we partied a little bit. Then you gave him a ride to Savannah, Frank."

— Rockstars and Executions —

Frank: "Thanks Mike buddy, talk to you later."

"The Coronado Connection got fucked up. This was some story: he taught Spanish at the high school and coached some sports team too—he got a couple of his students to deal for him—and they got big. The Coronado Connection. They were bringing in everything from Thailand, which meant they were bringing in a lot of stuff, and they had some stuff coming in from Cuba. They were guys that I was doing a lot of business with, and we made some friends who they were doing business with, so when the Coronado Connection went dead we just adapted. The cockfights in Miami, that's where I got tied up with the Cubans. This was the same time the weed from Mexico wasn't really available anymore, because they were spraying that paraquat shit, they were taking out all the fields in Mexico, so I was pretty hot to get the marijuana from Cuba—then it became cocaine.

"The cocaine started for me when I got into a little fight with the personal security guy from Electric Light Orchestra. I had to show him my gun to clean up a little confusion, and at the time, I had the connection for Quaaludes too, so he said, 'Hey, aren't you the guy with the ludes?' The rock and roll acts were always asking for the ludes, and then coke started blowing up, and so this guy who did security for ELO asked for coke and says, 'Man, you can make so much more money selling that shit.' So, I did. I went back to the Cubans."

Frank settled in Miami later in life, as he is very quick to point out this consisted of living in a four-story condo on the waterfront with a girlfriend who is very blonde. Frank shows me videos of him winning weightlifting contests recently. In the video of the competition a wildly animated Frank is introduced over the loudspeakers as The Florida Man. He lives it up, laps it up, lifts it up, and drops it.

— Andrew Mallin —

A phone call from his girlfriend—she is in Mexico. He greets her with "Happy Valentine's babe, and I'll call you back, I'm with the writer man."

I go to leave, and Frank insists on accompanying me into the sunlight outside the house, him demonstrating breathing techniques.

Day Two

Kathleen

"I don't know when college became a reality, but the first step was winning a ten-thousand-dollar national merit scholarship. Then Yale reached out. I finished Magna Cum Laude at Yale, but, PHEW, when I started I was freaked out, all these kids had these private educations. A kind teacher lent me a copy of *Ulysses* and a couple other books, and I was a reader. I caught up. I figured out how to stay afloat. I got a full ride to Columbia.

"I knew the death penalty was racially biased. Any student is going to be influenced by a trusted professor, and I had a great one who hoped someone could help the innocent who were being sent to die. I got my first guy off death row while I was still his student.

"Want to know how I became a hot commodity lawyer? A doctor with some legal background came to the firm and said, 'I need your help suing Medicare because Medicare is holding back the scientific community by overly restricting what new treatments could be covered by Medicare.' So, I sued the federal government, and the judge ruled that the federal government had to create a medical review board for Medicare where citizens, companies, and others can state their case for (the) public record.

"Well, small medical device companies saw what I did with Medicare, and all the business came flooding in—they wanted me to fight for their devices to be covered. It was the compromise I made with myself: I got all types of different things covered by Medicare; this kept me away from having to represent any of the big industrial or chemical clients; and I wanted to make partner bad.

"Before George Stephanopoulos was on CNN, he was Chief of Staff for (President Bill) Clinton, and I thought he was the cutest guy ever. I joined a gym because I heard he worked out there.

"I couldn't make a relationship stick as a lawyer. You're never around. Way over three-thousand hours a year billed, I was never around, so it wasn't a big deal to me. I did some dating, but I never had an interest in having a family or slowing down. I worked.

"In my pro bono work for the innocence cases on death row, I began to work with Barry Scheck. He'd been part of O.J. Simpson's defense team, and he ended up starting the Innocence Project. Barry is not everyone's cup of tea, but I think he did some good.

*****

Frank

"When Lou Villar was arrested in 1981, he tried every fucking thing. He tried bribing the judge, he bribed the DA, he bribed congressmen. They still sent him to Terminal Island, and once he was there he turned state's witness. Twenty-five members of his crew—the Coronado Connection—

just gone. I drank, I did coke, I've hurt people—but it's not about me hurting anybody or killing anybody; it's not about that. It's about the money, so you shut your fucking mouth.

"I met Mama the Colombian at the cockfights in Miami. She liked me. You gotta understand there weren't a lot of faces that looked like mine around that scene, so I kind of stood out. I didn't really smoke weed— it messed with my focus— and I didn't drink much around serious people because I had to be on the mark. None of those things were for me. I'm more the guy who wanted to work out and likes to work out more than anything, you know what I mean? It makes me feel good. Anyway, Mama was getting out of her car or maybe getting in her car, and she was yelling how her fucking gun didn't fit in her car, and I said she needed to get a bigger car. And brother, she laughed. I knew about her from Pete and them, so it probably wasn't smart to say boo, but she thought I was alright for a gringo.

"I'm used to taking care of just me, but now I'm taking care of Kitty (Kathleen Behan). Taking care of Kitty is like my cardio, and in case you didn't know, power lifters, we don't like to do cardio. But this is what I do, I train her in breathing techniques, I train her in moving her body, bring her body alive. I want her to walk a hundred yards by herself. I want to beat back what's beating at her. I want her to be free to stand up when she wants.

"The oldest was Stanley, then my father and his twin sister, then brothers OC, Junior, and Luther. All of the men went into the service at one point. My memories are of them coming home from war a little bit rich, like they had some extra money for once. My father reminded me of Frank Sinatra, Ed Sullivan; he was a smooth son of a bitch. This is all happening ten miles from the Navy Yard. Next thing you know, Korea is happening and things are happening again. Tractor trailers and cars—everything is new, everyone has something new. We were one of the first families in our subdivision with a television. We lived a couple hundred yards off the railway line, which was bringing in coal and all kinds of ship fuel. I can remember the coal dust.

"My father got into trucking, and him and his brothers got into pulling hot loads. He would get pulled over frequently for trucking moonshine. The navy boys would drink all the moonshine you could get into town. Before refrigeration trucks, they had these tractor trailers they'd have to get in and push the ice in and all this shit, and this is a business that's mostly gangster-driven. The trucking industry in New York and Boston was serious gangster shit. When I was six or seven years old, I would start taking trips with my dad. My brother was thirteen when he got killed by two drunks driving, and the trips stopped.

"Up until then, my dad and his brothers were doing pretty well. When I was maybe four years old, my dad had built that house on the *cul-de-sac*. This is in Bowers Hill, a development, mostly Polish. Dad built a brick home, which was a big deal back then. It was wall-to-wall carpeting inside, which was also a big deal back then.

"It's not like now. Back then, all the bars were sorta hidden on the shitty streets; there were not any bars on the high street. I started private Catholic school when I was six, and I would get out of there and walk through this Polish neighborhood to this little place, like a convenience store you'd call it now. It wasn't a bar because this was on the main drag. So, this store had a jukebox, and I fell in love with rock and roll. I'd feed coins into that thing, and they'd be talking away in Polish all around me. It was a lot of fun as I remember.

— Andrew Mallin —

"My father would go on his trips, and he would say 'You're the man of the house now.' I was the oldest boy in the family, of the next generation, and I think that kinda fucked with my head. I felt like I had to be tough. I'm not blaming my father, that's just the way it was back then. All my uncles and aunts lived around the corner, we were tight.

"I was young, and I felt like I had to be tougher than I was. Back then, my parents both smoked, everyone smoked, and I got a bit of asthma. This was right around the time my brother got killed. I don't know, it was a lot for my father.

"Elvis complimented me on my sideburns. I had huge sideburns when I was a kid. I'd hit the speed bag and the heavy bag, then go to the bandshell. Once I'd made the connection through the bikers, I was bringing marijuana with me to the venues. Wasn't long before I was moving a lot of drugs there. I had one uncle who was a cop, and him and my other uncles had taught me how to get the cops on your side. You start with the patrol captains. 'Hey Captain Joe, I need two officers on this door this weekend.' 'OK, Frankie.' And I'd ask them, 'How's your family doing? How many tickets do you need for backstage? How many front door tickets do you want? How many t-shirts of the band you want?' And they understood that I might need some help if there's a fight that's starting or whatnot, and I think, 'Hey, I gotta go kick some ass.' Look, I can kick some ass, but I'm a guy in a black t-shirt and I have big facial hair and I look rough and tough, but I also look like someone you can fuck with. I'm just some punk kid. A cop is a cop. In any setting, when roughnecks see a cop in uniform, there's some more math they gotta do. Usually, that's enough to calm shit down. And then if they weren't moving, if they weren't chilling out, then a cop or two would take their clubs and go to work. No assault charges against me,

Rockstars and Executions

it's just cops doing their job. And in addition to all the tickets and all the free shit, I'd give each cop a hundred bucks after the show. Each man, a hundred bucks, crisp. The captain was two hundred bucks. I was moving so much marijuana, it was well worth it.

"This is at the Virginia Beach Dome. That's the first venue I worked, and it was always my best. This is less than thirty miles from where I worked at the Navy Yard. The first two shows I did were Jimi Hendrix and Stevie Wonder. What separated me from the pack of gangsters who knew a rock and roll act or two was this place called Foreman Field. It was this outdoor venue right next to Old Dominion University. Then there was the Norfolk Arena, which was right downtown in Norfolk. I walked James Brown onstage in 1969 at the Norfolk Arena. I think I was the only white guy there.

"I walked Elvis onstage at the Hampton Coliseum in Newport News. The man who was the manager for The Beach Boys was also managing Elvis' concerts at the time, and I had supplied some things to The Beach Boys; they recommended me to Elvis's manager, so I met Elvis. That was in 1974, and then I met Elvis again in '76. I wasn't really noticing his appearance the first time I met him, he seemed alright. But the last time I saw him, holy shit Elvis looked bad. He fired one of his backup singers right there behind the stage. He was pissed at her, I mean pissed. He could barely breathe deep enough to work up the anger to fire this poor girl. He was sweaty, fat as fuck, and couldn't keep his shit straight. He was pissed at her because he couldn't sing anymore.

"When it comes to preparing for the big rock shows I kept the drugs on me. I had to be ready to help 'em out: Quaaludes, weed, Thai sticks, hash, uppers, downers. Then in '78 or '79 everything switched, overnight it felt like. The only thing I needed to have ready on me was a shitload of cocaine.

"Everything was arranged—not the drugs (laughs)—but everything else was arranged over the phone and over the fax. I would sign off on providing security for event X, Y, and Z, (send) the paperwork to whoever is managing, usually someone on the music label side of the business. By January, you would know the schedule for the whole year. Then, the week of shows I would gather up what guys would be working that night, what cops could work it, and which captain I'd be dealing with.

"Billy Joel was funny as shit. His first wife wanted to fuck me. Billy Joel loved cocaine—loved it—but he never wanted to pay for it. Billy's rough-looking on even his best day, but he's mostly fine. He's a funny guy, but don't let anybody fuck with his hair. Even way back in '84, '85, Billy Joel was looking a little rough. It's usually the road manager or somebody with the band who would come to me looking for the drugs. Instead, it's Billy Joel's first wife in a fully see-through outfit, top to bottom see-through, and she was eager to party. Then after the concert, we'd be there all night long rolling around until the morning. Seven a.m. was usually when we'd close it down.

"Bruce Springsteen is easy to do. He's a depressive, he's never too much trouble. So, I would show up the back stage and be ready with my flashlight—that's part of my gig; I would lead them out onto the stage with my little flashlight. I'd ask, 'You stretch?' Bruce Springsteen wouldn't say anything. He just nodded, jeans tight enough to rip apart. Bruce was a cool dude, he kept it cool. He knew, you just say 'Hey, I need Hammer,' and he knew I'd be there. That I was a cool dude—that I kept my wits.

"I would have to go into limos, motel rooms, into shitty rooms, and pull these artists out of these shitbox hiding places where they're shit scared of going on stage. The promoters and managers would try, and then they'd send in the guy who sold them the fucking cocaine. And my nickname was Hammer to a lot of those guys, and I was able to pull and talk people into doing shit. Bruce Springsteen never pulled that shit.

"The Colombians had the coke; by the ton they had it. The Cubans were bringing it in. They would sell me ten kilos, or they would front me the ten kilos. I would then call my girl at one of them health food stores and ask if she had what I needed. Mandothol—I think that's what they were called—that's the shit they could sell at that store and which I cut my kilos with. (The anti-caking agent Mannitol is frequently used for cutting cocaine.) I would say, 'Honey, I need more than we can ring up,' and that's how ten kilos of raw becomes twenty.

"I grew up near enough farms and I saw roosters, but I never saw anything like the cockfights. The cockfighting room was huge. It was in this big-ass building about the size of a football field. There was a big fucking fence all the way around this site. There was only one entrance. You drive through this gate, and there's three guys with Uzis peering into the car. That's where I met Gilbert with his two-door Mercedes; I still remember that car. Gilbert Hernandez and his brother Pete, well, they kind of became my partners. People put us together. See, the cockfight was in the middle of this big-ass room, and the point of it really is that it's like a country club for gangsters. There's the cockfight ring and you can bet and have a good time, but then there's plenty of space to walk away and have a private word. I went from marijuana to cocaine real fast after meeting Gilbert and Pete.

"I had to be alpha. I just had to let you know that I wasn't to be fucked with, and so I met all these people around this cockfighting pit and the little stands of seats around the fight. There was the guy there who could sell you a Ferrari or Mercedes. There was a guy there who had boats falling out of his ass. There was the guy who could get you any kind of Lamborghini you want.

"There was one guy who bought a white Ferrari from me. Now, everyone had these things in red—everyone. Then, I had this special favor to do and I did it: I found this guy, this Bad Motherfucker, a white Ferrari. The feds eventually seized the thing in Switzerland of all places. Anyway, this bad motherfucker picks up the white Ferrari from me. I had to get the thing through people in Luxembourg; it was a whole fucking deal. And keep in mind, I could've gotten him three red Ferraris down the street. So, what does he do? I deliver the white Ferrari, and he paints it red. I nearly blew my shit. Sincerely, I nearly blew a gasket with someone you don't do that with, over a car being painted red. But the deal was a good one, as he needed work done and he was paying in kilos of raw."

Frank calls Delbert Pickett (name changed) and asks him to tell me about Elvis.

Delbert: "I started my business back in 1973 in Greensboro, North Carolina. This is kind of a weird story, you sure you want to hear it?"

Frank: "Go on, brother."

Delbert: "Well, I had just started this jewelry business—the rock and roll security thing was a side thing for me—and when I started the business I was in a hole in the wall. You had to go up some back steps to find my office; it was a mess. There was a restaurant downstairs across the parking lot, and so I ended up spending a lot of time down there. I was actually friendly with the Freemans, the folks who ran the restaurant, because I had gone to high school with their kids. Now, it was pretty well known by them that Elvis was seeing a young lady in Greensboro. He was around a lot, and he loved that country food. One day, Mrs. Freeman comes over to my table and says, "Elvis just called from down the street. He lost a diamond from his ring. Can you possibly fix it?"

"My store is upstairs; seriously, nobody could find it. So, I offered to just fix it real quick. He could wait in his white limo, which has pulled up outside. He was cool as could be though and said, 'I'll roll with you.' So, I walked Elvis Presley up these rickety stairs into the most pissant office you've ever seen. It even smelled bad, and he just sat there shooting the shit. He asked me to make him a couple more pieces of jewelry—he liked these big belt buckles I'd done up with diamonds and stuff.

"Well, a couple weeks go by, and he's still seeing this young lady, and he keeps coming over and hanging out at my jewelry store. I was sitting there like, 'Holy shit man, I've seen all your movies.' But mostly I couldn't get over how bad he looked."

Frank: "Do you remember when we swung by on the Billy Joel tour?"

Delbert: "I've done over a hundred shows, most of them with Frank. Billy Joel was the man. When Billy came to Greensboro back in '78, he was the headliner. Friends and Billy had gone riding motorcycles that day. They came by my jewelry store, so they said, 'We're about to do some sound checks.' I sat there on a folding chair on the stage next to a business-sized piano. Billy comes out and says, 'What do you want to hear?' I said he played a mean Beatles song one time—Frank had told me about it. Billy Joel played Beatles songs for the next half hour, not another soul on stage. A personal concert of Billy Joel playing the Beatles."

Frank: "Wasn't one of the first times we met at that Mick Jagger party with the fireworks?"

Delbert: "Yeah. Frank and my brother were good friends; we were all doing the rock and roll thing. One night my brother calls me up and says, 'We're going to a party at Mick Jagger's hotel room, you want to come?' Jagger was so stoned when I got there, so fucked up, you could wave your hand right in front of his face and he wouldn't move a muscle. A few minutes after we got there Jagger started throwing up, and I look at my brother and say, 'I think it's time to leave.'

"I remember the first time I met Charlie Daniels. I was a huge fan. He reached out and shook my hand and said, 'Your name is Delbert?' I said, 'Yeah.' He said, 'Don't tell nobody.' He said, 'Delbert McClinton is 'bout to walk in.' When he did, he looked from him to me, all solemn, and he said, 'Delbert, meet Delbert.' And he thought that was the funniest thing ever. I gave him the hat he is wearing in *Urban Cowboy*. Charlie wears this hat with CDB buckles on it in *Urban Cowboy*."

Frank: "That was the first time I ever seen Charlie Daniels ask for coke. Alright brother, talk to you real soon."

I ask Frank what he thinks of the rock and roll industry on the whole: did he enjoy being some part of it?

Frank: "The guy I liked the most was Jerry Lee Lewis; he was the real deal before there was a real deal. Look at Sly and the Family Stone footage, then look at what Prince was doing on his Purple Rain Tour. I worked that tour. Prince took a lot of what Sly and the Family were doing and turned it up a couple notches. Paul McCartney was the guy who knew how to make the most money. Who was the biggest star I ever met, who felt the biggest? Well, it would probably be Michael Jackson, but do you remember Shaun Cassidy? He was a movie star, teen idol; then he becomes a recording artist.

— Rockstars and Executions —

He played a couple shows, and holy shit, I've never seen women lose their shit like that. I mean, women liked to lose their shit at big rock concerts, but for Shaun Cassidy? They lost. Their. Shit.

"The first time I met The Eagles was when they came to Greensboro. The promoter gives me a handful of backstage passes, and he says, 'Give these to good-looking women.' There's a cafeteria next to the arena. So, I'm waiting at this table in a cafeteria, and these girls are all smoking pot and hash and we're waiting under this one light. Don Henley walks in with this other guy—it's Glenn Frey—and Don and this other guy walk over to the jukebox, ignoring me, ignoring all these beautiful women. Don Henley and Glenn don't talk to me. They tell their manager, and he comes over to tell me the message: I got to go. They don't want me there, just the girls. I say, OK, fuck it, what do I care? I get up to go and say, 'Ladies, I'm leaving and y'all have fun.' They go, 'Wait, what? Why?' 'Well, the rockers over there are excited to meet you and not me, so I gotta scoot,' and Henley and Glenn Frey are still acting like the jukebox is just the most fascinating fucking thing they've ever seen. And so, I stand up and I start to leave, and the ten girls all stand up at the same time. They look at the manager, who's come running, to say if I can't stay they don't want to stay. So, the manager puts his arm around me, and then on my other side is Don fucking Henley, the world's friendliest all of a sudden. He's looking at my belt buckle because I'm wearing this big, gold eagle belt buckle. And he likes it. 'Where'd you get that?' he asks me. I said, 'My buddy made it; that's what he does. Some buddies are jewelers when they're not doing this security stuff.' Well, for the next half hour the girls couldn't even get a glance. These guys just wanted to talk eagle belt buckle jewelry.

"They were adamant they needed the belt buckles before their Japan tour. They ordered seven. I shipped them from Greensboro to California."

I've seen The Eagles wearing those belt buckles in pictures. I'm not entirely certain about the rest.

Frank: "When it comes to hair and makeup, Mick Jagger was one of the worst for being insecure about his look, and always needing more makeup. David Bowie was probably the furthest out there, along with Prince. Prince was a weird bird. You'd think he would like guys, but he was about the women. Weird bird.

"At the end, I got real fucking goofy. Too much, too much exposure to crazy shit. So, I got this government offer on a Friday, and it was a jewelry type thing—drug money intertwined with some other stuff—and I was so fucked up with Customs agents all around me. They had me square. I called my sister in Richmond and had her drive a van of hers up to DC. I was in a hotel room. My main guy was in jail. I was about to go away; I could see the end of the road. I got as far as Georgia before the van gave out, then I kept going. I got that jewelry all the way to Miami. The jewelry was worth one-point-five million; they offered me a hundred and fifty grand cash. So, I called the federal agent from a pay phone. This Special Agent, his name was Ozzy; he was flipping out, screaming, 'Where the fuck are you?' I said, 'Oz, I made a mistake. I got fucked up in my head, and I went back to gangsterland. I went to Miami with the jewelry. I was gonna sell it and leave the country.'

"Ozzy and I are still friends. He was pissed, but I got back to DC before Monday—according to his bosses I'd never left. Far as they knew I never took the jewelry. I was willing to play ball with my main guy in the federal joint already. I took the deal the Customs guys offered."

My evening notes: Both days have begun with Frank pushing me to talk with Kathleen before spending any time with him. He'll say something about talking about good stuff and then will close the door behind him on us with words of encouragement. He does not coddle her, his attitude towards her appears wholly driven by her goal to walk on the beach unaided.

Physically Frank is clearly still capable of hammering me through the pavement. He's shown me the house where he and Kathleen live. His bedroom is filled with trophies and books on sex; it's like an eighth grader's dream come true. He answers the questions I expect him to dodge without hesitation. For all men, a grain of salt is best taken when listening to tales of the money they made, the women they dated, the homoerotic feelings they definitely never had, and so on. He offers conflicting events for when, where, and why he's been arrested in his life.

Day Three

Kathleen

Kathleen has climbed the stairs this morning. The triumph is still being celebrated as I knock, am admitted, and get my laptop out. When I'm ready, she points to a framed *Time* magazine cover behind her.

"I went to Mississippi because I had been working in Louisiana after hearing things about people dying at Angola, the big prison there. And in Mississippi, guys were getting sentenced without even getting to see a public defender, tried without an attorney—mostly poor, mostly rural, and mostly Black people that couldn't put up a defense because they didn't know the first thing about what a defense was. So, they would just sit there and take a thirty-year sentence from the judge.

"These are mostly men. Down South they don't really keep the women in jail; if they had kids they were pretty much gone, no matter the crime. Now, *Gideon vs. Wainwright* . . . " [She quickly explains the ruling; the case involved a white defendant sentenced to five years for breaking and entering in Florida. It led to courts being required to provide poor people legal representation for any serious crimes. It also cast doubt on rulings where the defendants had not had any legal representation.] " . . .

so, I said, let's pick the three poorest counties in Mississippi because we figured they'd be the worst. We went in and did some depositions of poor Black guys in prison who had been sent there without a fair trial, we gathered the evidence, and we sued the governor of Mississippi. Nobody was paying for this, this was on my time. I had squared with the firm by taking on corporate clients and having the Medicare line of work. What happened next shocked me; Mississippi admitted in our lawsuit that they had fucked up, that men were put on trial without reasonable defense. The state allowed us to reach out and if they wished, set these men up with public defenders. The men who had been sentenced were eligible for re-trial.

"Jimmy Dennis was in prison in Pennsylvania for a murder he did not commit. Jimmy had heard about me from some publicity around the *Gideon* thing. Jimmy contacted me, and I visited him on Death Row to interview him. My bullshit meter worked pretty good back then. Jimmy was a member of a gang that was up to no good, but Jimmy had not committed that murder. I knew after the first time we talked that he was deep in the shit. He was an innocent condemned to die. I created a team of young lawyers who researched his life and the case, we started fresh. Jimmy had an alibi, which was asserted at trial, but because his alibi was another African-American, the jury didn't rate it, simple as that. I knew what I owed Jimmy Dennis. He had to earn a fair chance to defend himself. This is America and he is a black man; he had to earn it. I was going to ensure he got the fair trial he'd been denied. I would get him off Death Row."

*****

— Andrew Mallin —

Frank

Frank walks in grumbling about living with Kathleen: how hard it is to find good nurses, how having her small dog around is different for him too. He's caring for others. He chuckles, remarking how it feels like he's building his karma back, that he never did anything like this before—you know, taking care of people.

"Uncle Stanley was the oldest boy of that family. After their father murdered their mom he became the father of the group. He married his sweetheart—I think it was the day after his parents died. Stanley took charge until the war started, and he went first because he was the oldest. My father was supposed to stay home and watch the family, but he joined up right after Stanley. My father was in Europe on D-Day Plus Three. My father's name is Frank, but they all called me Little Frankie, never Frank Junior. My father's headstone is in Portsmouth; he died in 1981.

"My son's name is Frank. Well, I have six kids with five different women. I have twins with one woman. She's a model in New York. I never hear from her. I knocked up the postmaster general of Virginia's daughter. I have one boy who's Jewish. She's a Jewish girl with a nice family, and my Jewish son, he's only thirty.

"Stanley was in the trucking business before he went, and when he got back from the war he got into the mirror and glass business. Lot of that to move around. Stanley was young, he was energetic, and he had a young family. The brothers didn't even ask if they worked for Stanley. It was just natural, they all stuck together. They were a family. Every time I go back, I go to see the graves in Portsmouth. I just stand there for a bit. It's good to be with them. Sometimes I get lost, and it's good that I know where they are.

"My father never talked about the war except one time—a guy asked him, 'Were you scared?' He said, 'Yes, everyone was scared.' He said he dug a foxhole so deep that he could barely see the top of it. Because he was so scared and digging gave him something to do.

"All of my uncles got into the trucking business except for Luther; he became a Navy lifer. He served in Korea too. I can still remember Luther walking in the back door in his uniform. Holy shit he was a cool dude. I can still remember, I was real young, but I can remember that feeling of when the guys from the neighborhood came back from Korea, and we had a big party. I remember the whole neighborhood partying. Maybe it's just because I was little, but I thought it was a big deal when Korea was over. That shit got more than a handful of neighbors killed."

Does the illegal stuff in the trucking business build slowly or did it happen all at once?

"It was the port. All of the goodies would come into the port. I can remember the garage of my parents' house: we had the whole stalk of bananas hanging up, sacks of potato, squash, watermelon, cantaloupes, all kinds of goodies."

Did Stanley or your father carry a gun while driving? "They all carried a gun.

"Truck Stops were all-night parties back then. They were 24/7 facilities for sleeping, taking a shower; truckers could rent a cot. This was in the era before the rest stop. You ate breakfast, lunch, and dinner at a truck stop. Most places, most eateries, don't have the facilities, the size of parking, for these trucks. So, they go to the truck stops, and it's a business 24/7. Something coming in, something going out, and always a party. Yea, my dad and all my uncles carried guns.

"Stanley died in a car crash. Maybe somebody owed him some money, so Stanley shot him, then the law came for him. He was different, way different. Stanley was known to taunt people, you know, with his gun out and shit. He had a different way about him. I learned a lot from Stanley, and things were way different then, people don't understand how different things were then. But I didn't just learn from Stanley, I learned what not to do. Never taunt somebody with a gun, or you have to use it. He died in a high-speed car crash, running from the law. I think I learned a lot that day. I was maybe eight or nine years old the day Stanley died. It was a big deal.

"I remember my father went to the car wreck. I was in the back of my father's car when he went to look at Stanley's car. It was the next morning; it was dark out still, and we drove to the wreck site. He thought Stanley hadn't lost control of the car. He thought somebody had been shooting at him, so he looked for blowouts and windows all shot to shit. I don't remember much, but he didn't find nothing. It was just a fiery wreck, which had been a nice car the day before, and my uncle was dead. Dad drove home, didn't say a word. We got home and it wasn't yet light out.

"After that, nothing changed except they sold Stanley's glass business to some guy who was friends with Stanley. He was a different kind of guy, like Stanley, and my father and his brothers didn't want any business with this friend of Stanley's. They were maybe a bit scared of him. They sold that business for cheap to that guy. And they kept trucking.

"Look, here's the deal, I had three jewelry stores, and they washed the money. All of the money went into the stores, and jewelry and more money came out. Virginia Beach area is big in the international diamond exchange business. One of the biggest jewelers in India became a business associate. I met him on Chic's Beach, and he moved a lot of diamonds. This is right before I moved to Luxembourg. I had to get to a place where they wouldn't extradite me right back here if they found me. I had a friend whose father owned the second-largest Ford dealership in Europe, and he was the one who told me about Luxembourg, and it was a place where the jewelry business and the car business were good. This friend had a cargo plane, Cargolux; that's how I went to Europe for the first time, me in the only row of seats in the whole plane and a cargo of cars behind me. They owned a Ford dealership, and they were doing well. They were shipping those pieces of shit on four wheels to Europe in the Cargolux and then bringing back mint cars. I remember what year it was because I bought satellite TV for my house in Luxembourg sometime in like '83 or '85. I ordered the satellite TV because I wanted to watch the Prince show. Prince did one of the first live TV events of a big concert.

"Sophie Barnock's. That was the name of the bar in Bowers Hill. Bowers Hill was this development, little neighborhood, with three sides fenced off and a big marsh on the other side, so if it came time to run, the marsh was always there. I had most of my cousins and friends from home working with me at one point. So, Sophie Barnock was the local bar, you know, and the woman who owned it, I don't know if her name was Sophie. She was a Polish woman, and this bar had ice delivered every day. They didn't have a refrigerator there, and this was maybe 1975. But all the cops hung out there, lots of off-duty cops, and it was state troopers during the day and locals at night. We learned a lot at Sophie's. Her son Ed was a pilot, and towards the end of my thing he would fly for me occasionally.

"So we had a deal to do, and my friend Ed is going to meet me and some Cubans at a little airport, and I'm going to drive my car home, and he is going to fly the plane to Portsmouth. There is an airport there that's three miles from my parents' house. I get to the little airport where we're meeting, and Ed has driven there in my brand new SES Mercedes, which was part of the plan, but he was drunk as hell. I slapped the shit out of Ed. I told him, I said, 'Ed, you're my friend, and I just slapped the shit out of you.' I was doing my Boss act. And I said, 'Ed, if I ever mess up, you slap me hard as you can. We're not gonna be stupid here.' He was fine with that. I got him to a little diner and pumped him full of coffee and eggs, then got him the fuck outta there. That plane couldn't hang around that runway for too long.

"Working in the ship yard was my entry into the marijuana business. I also got more into doing the security for the rock and roll not long after. All the big ones that came through Virginia. And I'm providing security, and I'm selling marijuana, or Thai sticks, or hashish, then Quaaludes, bennies, then I'm selling cocaine, maybe some heroin too. When you're working a really big rock and roll show it's maybe two or three separate deals. First, the band buys the drugs. Or the manager would buy all the drugs for the guys in the band. And the road crew buys drugs. Then there were all the fucking people who came to the shows. A lot of time the band members were a couple different transactions because, you see, they didn't want the other guys in their band to know what they were buying. The worst for this was The Rolling Stones. They'd come in one by one and act like nobody could know about what they were buying, like it was a state secret. Meanwhile, hey Mick, we can all see you."

Describe the ten minutes before a really big show.

"You can feel the energy rising, everyone is getting set. It's like the football players running out of the tunnel, it's sort of like that. Everything is in motion. The band members are getting themselves right, outfits and everything else. Charlie Daniels would gather anyone going on stage together, he would always gather them up and say, 'Stay. Tight. Stay tight.' Each band had their own way of getting together, and then they would go. The huddle was about pumping their energy up because they knew what was about to happen when they walked on stage. Once a show starts, it doesn't stop. For a lot of the bands the first couple songs were chosen specifically to warm up the band, warm up the vocal cords, warm everything up. Some bands wrote songs specifically for warm-up songs for concerts. Some of them drank alcohol, some of them drank water or whatever, some of them wanted to smoke a joint, and some of them wanted a bump, some of them wanted any of those things during the show. The tours are where people start falling apart because that's when the drinks and the drugs happen every night. I mean just look back thirty years ago—if the Rolling Stones carried on acting like that, none of them could possibly still be alive today. And that's what happens to so many of the bands, they lose their lives on the road. Even if they come home alive, they're not long for this world."

Describe the ten minutes after a really big show ends.

"Well that's when the vehicles are all lined up and pointing out of the venue. We got towels ready for them. A lot of them would not want to go backstage again or back to the dressing room. They just wanted to go and get the fuck out of there. A lot of the rock and rollers wanted to get back to a hotel room or bus or whatever and just take a shower, then they would go out. Some of the acts didn't have to shower after, but most serious rock and rollers are sweating their tits off on stage. Some of the acts, like The Who, they needed some serious time to come down from the energy of the big shows. They didn't want to see anyone, they didn't want to talk to nobody, they didn't want to see no women. They just needed time to decompress. I remember they would have this British food, little packages of food that didn't sound good to me—didn't look good to me either—but they would have those little tokens of home I guess you'd call them. Weird cookies and the like. Some of the bands would have managers or friends going into the crowd after the show, looking for beautiful women who are interested in hanging around. That was usually going on, but I was usually more focused on getting the acts to where they wanted to go quick and then gathering up all the goodies and whatnot that I had going during that show: money, drugs, leftover shirts, leftover whatever.

"Selling to the crowds was easy, and it was never me. The t-shirts made money in two ways. A band comes to town, you know in advance, you make some t-shirts with the band name or whatever on it, you walk around the venue selling shirts. I would give the t-shirt guys half of whatever they made. It was a way to try and keep them honest because you would give them a couple ounces and they'd sell anything down to grams and the pills and whatever else, and man, we made money off the t-shirt thing. The other big source of revenue at a big show was selling backstage passes. Five hundred to a thousand for a really big act. Sometimes, it felt like I was making more money than the acts that came to town.

"You've got the limos, the vans, the catering services. There was one catering service for the band, one for the road crew, and then one for the guys who tune guitars and physical setup. I delegate the food thing to different food vendors. Some groups toured with their own chef. The country music acts were less picky, but they were still picky—good barbecue, that kinda thing. But even back then, you'd get this country music guy from nowheresville and he wants sushi, he won't eat nothing but sushi. Alright, fine, add it to the bill.

"Keith Richards would smoke cigarettes pretty much all the time he was doing a show. On stage, he'd always have a cigarette drooping from the corner of his mouth. There was coke in the cigarette every time. Smoking cocaine cigarettes, that's hard shit. That's like freebasing. And he's just out there. I've seen what alcohol does to people, I saw it from a young age. I'm the kinda guy who can have one beer, maybe two, and that's it. I liked the weightlifting contests. I stay away from the sugar, and no beer within two months of a competition."

Frank calls a friend named Jay Bell and asks him what year they met on the Billy Joel tour. Was it Jay who got Frank the job working the Prince tour?

Jay: "That was 1981. Billy Joel. Bill was way ahead of me at Hicksville High School. I graduated high school in 1976, my first work in security was in '79. I got into kickboxing when I was young. I won some WAKO (World Association of Kickboxing Organizations) kickboxing championships: Germany in '87, Venice Italy in '91.

Frank: "This is one of the meanest motherfuckers on this planet. Jay is one tough dude. He was my collection guy. In that line of business sometimes you got people who owe money or who owe other things, and we'd send him in, say 'Jay, our guy is going to be coming out of this bar with his girl.' So, Jay would go up to the guy and act all sissy, put a lot of fruit in his voice, and compliment the guy's girl. Then he'd wait for the guy to swing or try to deck him, and then he would go. He could go. Once Jay was done hitting the guy and the guy was on the ground, he'd continue in his sissy voice 'You owe some people some money, yes you dooooo,' like in a singsong. Man, he made us laugh with that."

Jay: "Sure, Frank."

Frank: "Hey, hey, tell the story man why you got fired from the Purple Rain tour, if that's cool with you."

Jay: (laughs) "Oh man, Frank, you got one kind of memory. Yeah, I remember."

Frank: "He was fucking Apollonia."

Jay: "We had some fun."

Frank: "Prince was pissed!"

Jay: "Yeah, it turned into a bit of a situation. I thought it was best to clear out of there."

Frank: "Prince is maybe five-foot-two. Jay is a big guy with the longest legs you've ever seen. Prince was an insecure fucker. Anyway, thanks brother man, take care of yourself."

Jay: (laughs) "Alright Frank, alright, you take care."

You mentioned a Federal Agent Ozzy yesterday? What did the end of the road look like for you?

Frank: "Let's just say this: I owe my life to them customs guys because they saved me. Bill Snouffer got put in the penitentiary. He was the bodyguard for Billy Joel, Ozzy Osbourne and Prince. He got arrested for cocaine trafficking, marijuana trafficking by the ton, some other shit. His cousin rolled over on him. Bill Snouffer was in Cancun, and he called me, 'Hammer, they're on to me, but my lawyer is taking care of me.' I said, 'Listen to me: stay in Cancun.' Bill says, 'Nah I'll beat the case.' This is after the Purple Rain tour. I was in trouble too. I told him to stay. I had one foot out of the country myself. I ended up in Kathmandu, Kashmir. Spent time in India. Anyway, I said, 'Bill, don't come back.' Well Bill landed in

— Rockstars and Executions —

Miami, and they arrested him right in the airport. It blew up, bad. Everything was everywhere, all about how the people around the rock and roll were trafficking, and it's all going bad.

"It was right around this time I went to see Whitey Durham in Greensboro. Whitey was a famous dealer. He was big time, and he was someone I had done some stuff for. I was laying low, he was helping. So, I'm staying there outside town, and it's me, him, a couple girls. He comes in my room one morning with the newspaper. It's got his name in it. It's all about what we been doing in rock and roll and jewelry and cars.

"Bill Snouffer made bail. I don't know how, I wasn't involved. So, what did Bill do? Keep in mind he is lost at this point, he's snorting cocaine all day long. Well, he got out of jail on the mother of all busts, and he goes to the newspaper guy who put Bill's name in the paper. He wasn't very polite, so the newspaper guy called the FBI and says, 'Hey, this guy just threatened me.' So now Bill is fucked. The feds picked him up and that was that. Pretty much all of the people in the business who knew Bill knew me. I had to get out of the country, there wasn't anything else to do.

"One of the last big deals I ever made was with this guy called Trucker. I had him meet me in Bowers Hill. I was hiding in my parents' basement that day. This guy was country as a motherfucker. I say, 'Let's go to the restaurant and get some food, then we'll get you setup and get you out of here.' I go in there and say, 'Have you ever eaten a lobster?' He goes, 'What's that?' So, this fucker has never seen a lobster. The girls there all know me because I'm a big tipper, and I say watch this fucker, do it up. So, I have them bring the bib, the whole show, and I have them bring out the biggest lobster I've ever seen. And this country boy—the guy's name was Trucker—is looking at me, and he wants to know how the fuck do I eat this thing? So, the waiters bring the little hammer. And this fucker takes the hammer and tries to beat the dead lobster to death. He was swinging the hammer—you know how that juice sprays?—and he is bashing that fucking lobster until it jumped. Then it went into the butter and you should've seen him light up. I used to work with guys who had tables at the best restaurants in Miami reserved in perpetuity; now I'm working with this fucking idiot.

"Panama Red and Thai sticks were the two most popular kinds of weed. There was that Oaxacan shit too, and hashish was always popular. But then sinsemilla came along, and that's all anyone ever wanted again. We cut the weed bales with RC Cola and Coca-Cola. It made that shit sticky. We would have a room, and we'd be tossing that shit like salad. I had the guys with spray bottles like you do for Windex; they'd be spraying and spraying the weed with RC Cola or whatever, and it made that shit extra sticky. The rockers, what do you think they thought? They thought it was sticky weed, lot of THC. And it was, but it was also a fair amount of RC Cola making that icky so sticky. Then I got a big batch of weed that looked like shit, and I remember I had my guys dye it, we basically painted that shit green. I think some people got sick, I never did that again.

"The other thing I came up with that you might call marketing was this (and let me tell you, it was a home run): I dyed cocaine. I dyed Peruvian Flake. This shit was beautiful. You rub it on your fingers and you could feel the oil on your fingers. The cocaine oil was so rich in these fucking flakes. So, I had an idea. We got food dye—pink, non-harmful—and we dyed this shit pink. I called it Peruvian Pink. Lightning bolt from the sky. Light spritz of dye, lay the coke out, let it dry out. The enemy of cocaine is sogginess, so spraying it was a dicey operation. But we got this coke and this shit was light pink.

"So, I got invited to the Volunteer Jam through some friends in the business. The Volunteer Jam is in Nashville, and it's a big deal for the country music scene—but also a ton of rock and rollers. And I brought my Peruvian Pink to Nashville. Put it this way. I went to Nashville in 2010. I went to an art show. I ran into this guy I ain't seen in years. I saw him, and he goes, "You're the fucking Hammer! . . .Hey, can you get me any of that pink?" That's how popular that shit was—near thirty years later people are still asking for it."

Hammer?

"Some people called me Big Arms, some called me Hammer, people in Miami called me Mister Loco. I remember Barry Manilow calling me an asshole. (laughs) Barry Manilow was gay and what happened there was he had his boyfriend with him on the road, and they were very particular; we didn't really like them. They were real snotty about their fucking clothes. Every day it was some shit or another about their clothes. So, we took Barry Manilow's boyfriend and hung him up in a closet . . ."

Now, when you say you hung him . . .

"I mean we hung him up by his coat with him in it, you know? It's not like he was hurt or anything. They didn't take that kindly though, him and Barry; they were peculiar. The Beach Boys were more my style.

"This wasn't in Virginia, this is me and John Campbell doing security for The Beach Boys on their tour. Some of the road crew was in the band's bus, but everyone else was in a limo. John owned the limo service, and he'd set them all up. Our job was me and John would go setup the next town. We had our own limo, he and I, and we would setup the next town, then do security at the event.

— Andrew Mallin —

"I met the band first day of the tour. Brian Wilson and I hit it off pretty good because he liked the drugs. The drummer, whose name escapes me, [it's Brian's brother Dennis Wilson] went on Johnny Carson one time, and he was so coked out he couldn't hardly talk. I admit, that one was on me."

I can't even wait a full minute. I interject to ask him if he ever asked the Wilson brothers about Charles Manson and that whole mess.

"I knew about the Charles Manson thing, but I never asked them about that shit. I don't think he wanted to talk about anything but drugs and women then.

"The drummer was Dennis Wilson, Brian Wilson's brother, that's right. So, Dennis comes to me and says, 'I need Quaaludes and some coke and some other stuff.' We meet them outside the venue, us in the limo and they're coming off the bus. And we're walking and talking as we go into the arena.

"Now keep in mind The Beach Boys toured with a psychiatrist and a therapist. Well, the therapist comes up to me—he's got the big man energy going—and he is fucking pissed. He's yelling at me, asking what did I give Dennis Wilson? Saying 'He's fucked, he can't do no show now, you idiot.' Then the psychiatrist comes up, and he is freaking the fuck out too because evidently Dennis Wilson has it in his head to find a jet plane and jump out of it without a parachute, to see what happens. Jumping out of a plane has become priority One-A for Dennis Wilson. So, we're standing next to this big display of shrimp on ice, it's on this big table, and the psychiatrist and therapist for The Beach Boys are talking to me like I'm an idiot, 'Why did you do this, why did you do that?' I cut them off. I said, 'Is he a grown man? Can he handle his shit or not? What the fuck are we talking about here?' They were pissed, yelling at me, and that's when I lost it. I said I'm doing them a favor even being here, I don't need this. So, I said, and I'll admit I wasn't that cool about it because on a big tour you have to put up with some shit, but I said, 'Do you see that ice display with shrimp all on it? How'd you feel about having your fucking heads planted through that ice and that table? You want that?' They scrammed, they got out of there.

"Brian Wilson came up to me. He says it's all good, and he's real calm. He is also high as shit. So, he says, 'Let's go get some fucking drinks.' Everything gets settled down while we're down the street at some shitty bar. And Brian is drinking triple martinis. You've gotta be kidding me. I'm trying to make the cutoff gesture to the bartender because I don't want that reputation of fucking up all these guys before a show, and I'm making a cutoff gesture to the bartender and Brian notices, and he's not pissed but he's not pleased either. He's real laid-back. He says, 'Hammer, I will tell you when I am done. I am not done before I tell you I'm done.' So, I'm like, 'Well, you're the Beach Boy.' He says, 'I'll let you know when I'm done.' I kept trying to order beers, but nope, it was triple martinis all afternoon. Somebody else had to come yell at him before he would leave the bar.

"So opening curtain time is getting close. We're back at the venue. When they're on-stage there's already another security guy who's watching after Dennis. The manager comes up to me and says, 'You're going up on stage with them. You're keeping an eye on Brian.' Turns out Brian has occasionally wandered off stage during the shows lately, and I'm going up there to keep him at the piano. So, he's sitting there playing the piano, show's going wild, and Brian just kinda stops playing. He just stopped playing. His head would roll back, and he would kinda gaze at the ceiling. This happened four or five times that show. So, I would go to Brian and pantomime playing the piano, with two hands up in the air like I'm playing a big piano. I'm jumping up and down like I'm a fucking kitty cat, making piano hands. I'm slapping my hands and getting him to look at me—play motherfucker! He just kinda smiled at me, so I pulled him over and gave Brian a master blaster."

What's a master blaster?

Frank holds his hands up, about a foot apart.

"It's a pretty big bump. It's like one big snort tube. It goes in both nostrils at once, and it only has one opening on the other end, so you'd get it up both sides of your nose. Brian played great after that. But Brian loved the Quaaludes; that shit puts a dent in you. I had one million Quaaludes at one time. I'll never forget. It was that same tour. I went on The Beach Boys' bus one time and it looked like they had all been poisoned, you know, or like they'd been gassed. People were lying down where they'd fallen. It looked like *Romeo and Juliet* or Jonestown. They were fine. Fucking Quaaludes."

Day Four

Kathleen

"I stopped drinking when I had my first strokes in 2013. I had tried quitting for years before then. I had my first virgin cocktails when I was six years old, putting maraschino cherries in a little soda water—it was very exciting. My first real drink was this horrible white wine. I kind of knew from the beginning, but when I went to Columbia it just hit me smack in the face: this was going to be my problem now. I didn't allow friends to know about my problem.

"I started working at Arnold & Porter, and they had an open bar in the office every day at five. It felt like getting a leg up in my career getting drunk every day after work. I went into treatment for about a month when I was a partner, then I went back to work. That's when I noticed we didn't even offer soft drinks at the company open bar. I had a boyfriend of a couple months then. He liked to sail and drink. He was also one of the top economists in the country. He didn't consider himself an alcoholic. One time he came to the treatment center I was in, picked me up to have lunch, and he had a couple drinks at that lunch. We broke up for good not long after.

— Rockstars and Executions —

"Have I told you about what happened at Angola yet? That's the Louisiana state prison, I worked with Blake on that one. Let me send him a note, see if he'll talk to you for me. I am done-in."

Day Four, evening: Blake Biles, partner at Arnold & Porter. Washington, D.C.

Blake: "We both worked at one of these very large law firms, and the great fortune of working at this firm is we have a history of doing pro bono work. Representing big companies pays for it all, of course. Early on, my view was that the industry viewed pro bono work as stuff like being on the board of a ballet or serving on the board of a charitable organization. But long before I got here Arnold & Porter was different. If you're asking me, it was created by a bunch of ex-New Dealers, among them a man named Clarence Gideon. He brought the case that protected the right to representation.

"Kitty and I came to the firm at different times, and as far as I could tell, we didn't have a single interest in common except our pro bono work. At that time there was no expectation of doing pro bono, and the firm entirely left it to us to pick and choose what to work on.

"We're very, very fortunate to be able to help. I have no sympathy for lawyers who say they have too much workload.

"Kitty and I are cut from different cloth, we are very different people. But we are very similar in the way we feel about compassion. It was only later that I learned about Kitty's childhood, how she had grown up. There are all sorts of stories about why you do things. Sometimes we have very good lawyers who are idealistic, and they'll say, 'I don't want to work for X and Y.' There can be a world between an idealist and a compassionate, driven person.

— Andrew Mallin —

"I'm seventy-five, and I'm still here, in part, because I get to work on affordable housing. You can deliver to tenant groups what you deliver to corporate clients, which is the full service with a lot of brainpower behind it. Smaller firms cannot do that, they do not have the resources. It means we don't have to worry if we can afford the extra deposition that might bear fruit or the extra hours to research—we can. I am unabashed to be very happy at where I work.

"I'm from Kansas. My dad was a Depression-era small businessman. I am a good lawyer. I know my shit, and I enjoyed what I did in my day job, but I always loved what we do in pro bono.

"It is an overstated perspective, but you normally get two different groups of people who do lots of pro bono work: young and old lawyers. For the young people, they don't have family or senior parents to take care of. They're eager, they are going to save the world. Younger employees are often willing to do more for others and are daring. Look, when I say 'family' it isn't all about immediate family. Family is broadly defined as whatever you do outside of the firm. But here at the other end of the spectrum—the geezers like me—our family life is pretty settled, and we can do a lot of pro bono.

"It's the people in the middle who are the next leaders. They generate funds by grant-making or bringing in clients, so those people have a stronger burden. Their practice needs to be building the place. That's where we worked, that is the environment.

"Kitty had a couple things going for her as a lawyer. It's not like we ever sat down and did an evaluation, but these are things I've picked up on over the years. Kitty has passion. It can never hurt to have passion, in my opinion, without knowing why, I could tell she was compassionate and passionate. Kitty was a leader. You can see how if you're a partner, you're smart, you know how to litigate on the things that pay the bills here, and you're doing pro bono, and you'll have people here who want to work with you. That is important. If nobody wants to work for you that tells me everything. Kitty always had a cadre of people who followed her. I thought she was always filled with idealism, but also realism, and people respond to the two put together. I never thought she was overly idealistic or became too much of a realist where she lost sight of her ideals. That is not to say the death penalty cases were easy. The work that Kitty took on was a huge source of tension in her life. She cared. She cared.

"I fell into affordable housing litigation fifteen years ago.

"There are all ways to put pro bono work in different silos. One question you'll always hear is, are you working impact cases or systemic cases? Can you possibly change the system, a la Gideon, or are you working a case that might in one case alone impact a number of people at once? I personally gravitated toward working with people, the impact cases. That was our work at Angola, Louisiana State Prison, where we represented a number of people by sticking up for the mental health rights of one inmate.

"What was happening at Angola was very much a systemic matter, but that's not why Kitty took the case and asked for my help. Kitty learned people were being hurt and abused, and when she learned about what was going on, she decided we were not going to stop until the killings stopped.

"In many ways, Angola is one of the last vestiges of a different South. It's a plantation, river and swamp on three sides, and you cannot escape from it. In those days, you would work out in the fields under the gaze of guys in aviator glasses. Who is to say when the bad days end, but in those days, Angola was under the thumb of a brutal warden and things were bad.

— Andrew Mallin —

"Some judges will—how to say this—let things work themselves out. Then there are other judges who will, as needed, have a receiver appointed and who will take charge of things in cases before him or her.

"There was just such a judge in Louisiana, which is how our story begins. There was a US judge in Baton Rouge who had a reputation for not taking any shit, so when he got word from somebody on the hush that there was a dramatic uptick in suicide at Angola, he set out to investigate. The uptick in deaths was so dramatic that they were running out of space to dig the graves. As if it's not bad enough being in Angola already. This judge appointed someone to investigate, and the investigator came back with what was going on. For cost cutting reasons, the administrators of the prison had cut back on mental health services—by cutting all mental health services. We don't have time today, but a great many of the incarcerated people in our jails are there because too often we do not have any other care to offer the mentally ill. Even if the services were minimal, these people had been cared for and there had been some understanding of their mixed ability as laborers. Not under that warden.

"Angola was run like a military. You were part of a unit, and if you acted out, everyone in the unit got punished. So, there were inmates killing themselves in droves rather than face the unchecked retributions of the guards or the other men of their unit. When the judge found out, he made sure there was a stink. I think it was the show *Frontline* that finally did a story on the big spike in deaths at Angola. People in our LA and Washington offices saw the story and said we have to do something, and Kitty's was one of the first hands to go up.

"A funny thing in life is you never know if the people who say we have to do something did something.

— Rockstars and Executions —

"To try and stop the deaths, we sued for civil rights violations, and the relief we wanted was the reinstatement of a psychiatric program.

"Our lawsuit was not to change the prison system or to change Angola. Our focus was on the lowest hanging fruit: mentally ill people who were killing themselves. The LSU psych department was quite capable of doing the work, but they were completely and purposefully underfunded. Because of the work Kitty Behan did, Angola prison now has a mental health wing, and the rate of suicide at the prison has never again come close to what it was. Though, I think, the warden survived it all.

"When I look at my career, I was a damn good cog and I enjoyed my work. Kitty was less a cog; she was much more a fighter. Because there is intense stuff going on out there and the way this world works, not everyone can fight for themselves.

"Roger Coleman, through DNA, has been proven guilty, and that was particularly difficult for Kitty. What it feels like to have fought for a man she thought innocent—it is hard not to feel like a sucker, and there are doubts, but then DNA, and I just know she took that real hard. I know she did not like Roger—not one bit—but she fought like hell for him because she felt it was the right thing to do.

"It is crushing to believe yet find the lie. Kitty was way in on her pro bono work, more than most people get, and I've heard people criticize that about her. My answer is, fuck you. I might disagree with people's passion, but I appreciated their passion. Of no person is that appreciation more true than of Kitty Behan, someone who was committed to being true to herself despite the obstacles. Now, before I go, I have one more thing to tell you.

"Kathleen Behan has a great belly laugh; it is spontaneous and true.

"Goodnight."

— Andrew Mallin —

*****

Frank

"My father was fourteen and my Uncle Stanley was sixteen when my grandfather killed my grandmother. Grandpa tried to kill his son Luther, then killed himself. I never knew what set my grandfather off. I called and tried talking to my uncles about it again recently. They were in their nineties. Even then it was still kinda hush-hush. I get not wanting to talk about it. My thing is I think my grandfather must've had too much pressure on him. It was 1934, it was probably the worst of the Depression, and he just had so much going on. He had six kids and he couldn't feed them. One of my father's brothers, an uncle I never met, got killed in a gas station over a gun. That was not talked about either. And the thing about my grandfather, he was a blacksmith, he worked with metal in the shipyards, he would get covered in lead paint, he was working with chrome shit, he was working with this and that—metals that can fuck with your head, lead and stuff. Plus, he was a drinker. Even through prohibition Norfolk was a wet town. Any time there is men in the service there is going to be bars, there is going to be prostitution, and there are going to be con artists.

"My father never once talked about my grandfather. Never—except once. I'll tell you what happened. We're going to a place over in Norfolk, and Dad is driving, and he was kinda gangster. He was in the trucking business. He liked to drive convertibles. So, we're driving to Norfolk, we're going over to this deli, and he pointed to a cemetery as we passed it. He said, 'Your grandfather is buried there.' He never once talked about my grandfather after that, not a word.

— **Rockstars and Executions** —

"I have a picture of my favorite car. At one time, I had twenty-three cars; I was a car freak. I loved these two Jaguars: one in green, one in yellow. Beautiful cars. But my favorite was my customized Ford Pantera. I lost them all when I went to the Seychelles. I went there because I had read in the *New York Times* how anyone worth over a million dollars wouldn't be extradited from there. I don't remember if that was true or not, but I went there and I lived on Mahé, La Digue, and Praslin. I didn't stay anywhere for too long the next two years or so.

"But you asked me about the scariest guy I ever put on the ground. The biggest were these two guys at an AC/DC concert. They were in the standing area right in front of the stage. They were just really fucked up. I hooked the first guy's leg and hit him in the face, then got the second guy with a fork. That wasn't scary though, that was just two big fuckers. I spent a day in the trunk of a car in Miami, that was scary.

"This was a deal where they had already brought the coke in on our shrimping boat, and I had to pay. Okay, no problem. I had sent two of my guys to drive the money to where we were meeting. It was way outside town; it was swampland and a dead-end road. I got there, and it was a bad vibe from the beginning. There was some confusion and, um, lack of communication. I said, 'I got my guys coming with the cash.' This was only the second or third time I had done business with these people. Back then, my drivers had beepers, so I paged the fucking idiots who were supposed to be meeting me with about a half million in cash. Well, nobody called me back, and I was standing there getting a bit nervous now because I don't really know these guys, and the guy says to me, 'Hey buddy, no hard feelings but if the money isn't here in five minutes I'm putting you in the trunk of your car, and your car in the swamp.' I said, 'Who the fuck is putting who in a trunk? Fuck you.' Then all the pistols came out, and I said, 'Well, I guess I'm getting in the trunk of the car.'

"Besides my clothes, I had a Rolex on. Miami is hot. I was sweating my fucking dick off in the trunk because not only was it hot, I was trying to use the edge of my Rolex to break out of the trunk into the backseat. Occasionally, they would come back close to the car and tap on the trunk and yell, 'Where is the fucking money?' and I would holler loud as I could that he is coming. I kept telling them my guy is coming in a shitty Ford, he'll be wearing a red hat that says Miami on it, and I fucking swear he'll be here. I could hear them laughing, then they fired off a couple shots. They started the car. I was still locked in the trunk with a busted Rolex, and I think that might have been that if that fucking idiot didn't show up then. I tell you now, he got lost; my guy got fucking lost. I nearly got killed because this guy couldn't follow simple fucking directions.

"They put a couple bullets near him too. Then, finally, the cash came out, and they took it, and we're good finally, and they're laughing again, and they're saying to me through the trunk that, 'Look, this was just business.; we're going to let you out now and you're just going to be cool as a cucumber.' So, they open up the trunk, and I'm sweating my ass off, and I've got half my Rolex wedged into the opening to crack open the back row of seats, and I flop over and hop out, and they back away to give me space, but the Uzis are in my face. And I point a finger in the guy's face who led the deal, and I pointed at him and I said, 'You could have at least given me a TV; it was boring as shit in there.' Brother, I tell you, they pissed themselves laughing."

Did you work with your guy in the red Miami hat ever again?

"Yeah. Those roads are confusing.

— Rockstars and Executions —

"You don't call them partners, but I was put together for business with Gilbert Hernandez and Pete Hernandez. They sometimes said they were brothers. Picture a room with wires hanging from the ceiling, the floor is dirt with straw on top. This is where we train the roosters for the cockfights. We chase them and we taunt them and underneath that dirt floor is the drugs. There was a big trapdoor and it was loaded up down there. There would be up to a hundred kilos of coke under that ring. We had an espresso machine there. We were rolling. Only one day there are two cop cruisers at the gates. There was all kinds of wood fencing and corrugated metal all around the place, and they're at the gate. I'm a wanted felon at that point, so I take off. I jumped a few fences. So, there are these bushes that produce a little fruit—they're everywhere in Miami; the fruits are real pretty—anyway, these things have thorns about two inches long. I am scooting and I'm hiding over there, bleeding out behind some bushes. I can see the cops, and I can see they're not arresting anybody, they're just there. I was wondering if they were just waiting for the wagon—you know, a big bus to carry everyone they bust. Finally, though, they just leave, and I'm not sure whether to try and go back or to try and make it across the swamp and get the fuck outta dodge. My associates start calling me from over the fence, 'Loco, Loco, you can come back,' and I'm like, 'Eh, maybe I just keep going across the swamp.' Cops stayed the fuck away from the cockfighting place usually, so I wasn't so hot on going back without an explanation, but I went back. And Pete is there pissing himself, saying, 'You're not gonna believe what happened.' Gilbert's wife had called the police because Gilbert had taken their son to the cockfighting place. So, she called and said there's a bunch of gangsters at so-and-so place. The police came out and did a little look around, but there was nothing to see, so they left. So, what do you think this meant for Gilbert's wife? Death.

"We had all had a bit of trouble from her beforehand, so we go, we get something to eat, and we talked to Gilbert about his wife. We all said this is the second or third time she's caused trouble, now she's involving cops. She's gotta go. I said, 'I'll take this one.' I said, 'Are you alright with that Gilbert?' He said alright. I didn't like this motherfucker. She's already cost me plus now she's just losing it. So, I said, 'Now Gilbert we're not going to stop being friends just because I have to kill your wife.' I said we're still going to be friends. So, I went to a sports equipment store and I got a metal bat.

"I didn't want to shoot her because she lived in a subdivision. I didn't want to make a stink. I said, 'I'm Mister Loco. We're all going to the penitentiary behind this bitch. Even if she never says anything again, there's just this nerve that's been struck, like she might fuck it up again, so okay.' Business is big. So, I get her movements in the day from Gilbert, and he tells me when she goes to the mailbox. He says she walks to the mailbox by herself at something like 6 p.m. Their little subdivision was gated, but she had to go outside the gate to get the mail. Gilbert tells me this and we split. There wasn't much bushes there, and I was trying to hide. It wasn't easy. This is dusk. I'm waiting for her, and I'm trying to hide behind these tiny-ass bushes, and I'm thinking this is fucked up, I'm not hidden at all. I wished she would come out later because she's going to see me. Then all of a sudden the gate opens, and it's Gilbert. Now, when Gilbert is doing cocaine or drinking he would wear a robe. So, Gilbert opens the gate, and he's got his robe on and he's high as shit. He's in a robe, and he don't see me so I must've done a better job of camouflage than I thought.

"So, Gilbert is in his white underwear and this purple robe. He looked

— Rockstars and Executions —

like a fucking nut because he's squinting, looking at the bushes, and going, 'Loco? Loco? Loco?' I didn't want to say anything. Finally, I called out and I asked him, 'When is she coming?' And he goes, 'Well, we gotta talk about that.' Understand, we are whispering loud as can be. I am stuck head-first in a bush, my ass hanging out, I've got a bat in one hand, and finally I just stand up to face him. Well, he's telling me that he's changed his mind, that we're friends, but that he couldn't go through with this. We are standing there like Keystone fucking Cops, the two biggest idiots in the world. He's high and he's in the stupid puffy purple robe, and he's going, 'Man, I love her. I love her, man.' I wasn't even that mad. I had to laugh. I was just like, 'Now you decide to tell me this.' I told Gilbert, 'They're not gonna be happy with you, man, your partners and their bosses.' So, I go to meet those guys, 'cause they were waiting for me in the spot where I was gonna come say it was done. Well, I had to go there and say, 'Gilbert changed his mind.' Thing were pretty touch and go for Gilbert there for a little while.

"A long time later, Gilbert's old lady got involved with an undercover cop, Gilbert got arrested, and his wife settled down with the undercover cop once Gilbert was in jail. She now owns a bunch of [popular chain of gas stations with a touch screen interface for ordering sandwiches]. They bought their first couple gas stations with cocaine money that Gilbert had stashed around their place. The undercover never turned that shit in.

"That was how a lot of things went: people come and go. Gloria Estefan was marred to this guy Emilio. They owned a recording studio not far from this restaurant the Hernandez brothers owned, and a lot of cocaine and cocaine money flowed through that recording studio. It was the next month after our argument about killing Gilbert's wife that Gilbert and I sold two kilos to O.J. Simpson."

— 68 —

O.J. Simpson sold coke?

"No, you idiot. O.J. did enough coke that two kilos was something he wanted, for himself. I sold to Dennis Franks too. You might not remember him, but he played on the Eagles and was buddies with Vince Papale. I was there when Dennis Franks met his wife. This was at the Playboy Club in Miami. Yeah, there was a Playboy Club in Miami for a while, and let me tell you, it was some kind of scene. Dennis ratted out some people when he got pinched, but he was a friend of mine before he fucked up.

"But you asked me about the toughest guy I ever put on the ground? [I had. Yesterday.] It was my martial arts teacher, and I was young. I was just coming up into the business, so at that time it was marijuana, and I was eighteen, nineteen years old. This guy, Les Mayhew, was a martial arts instructor at that National Armory place in Norfolk, and this Les knew I was a boxer, he knew I could kick. We had maybe twenty-five people in there and we would go through the moves. Kung Fu was the most popular back then, and Kung Fu was a shitload different from street fighting where you just go. I remember I had a '69 GTO. I always carried a gun on me. So, I'm in there at that National Armory, and Les invites me to train with these guys. I could fight, but I wanted to learn how to fight on the ground too. There were all kinds of special forces guys who trained there, so we learned grappling, different hand moves, different moves, okay?

"It went on for maybe three-to-six months of good training, and Les would use me as the example. We would do drills like Bull in the Ring. I could see it coming that Les wanted to use me to show off. He had me take pictures where I was holding him over my head. It started to feel like I was his pet. So, we'd train every night from 7–9 p.m. So, I'm there one night, and we do Bull in the Ring drill. I remember this guy, Fred. He worked on a beer truck, he could kick my ass. Fred was a bad motherfucker. I grabbed him one day and told him he was better than me and better than Les because he was. I said, 'You're just lacking confidence.' I said that and about two weeks later, I do the Bull in the Ring. Les Mayhew calls himself into the ring, and he's an alpha guy who wants to show off and be admired. Maybe he heard me talking to Fred. Well, I'm an alpha guy too. In the Bull in the Ring, you're supposed to kinda pull your punches. Les wasn't pulling shit. The first couple times I thought maybe he made a mistake. Then he did it again, and I said, 'Motherfucker, aren't we supposed to be pulling our punches?' He said, 'What, can't you take it?' Well, I just about lost it. He's kicking the shit out of me, and I'm going for his eyes. The lights went out for me, and I was trying to get him any way I could, and we got out of the ring, and he put me in the wall. You know, put my head into the wall. Well, I lost my cool. I went out to my car. I was still all heated. I grabbed my .45, I went back in and held it to Les's head in front of a bunch of guys. I said, 'You deserve to die motherfucker. You're supposed to be a teacher. You're not supposed to be a fucking show-off, you're supposed to be a teacher.' But I didn't want to go to jail; I got out of there. I stopped going to the armory to train, but it got smoothed over. An uncle helped me clear it up.

"The toughest fight I ever had though wasn't with a human. A guy that was an associate of mine—he and his wife would sometimes drive cocaine for me—I went to see him late at night at his house. This is just outside Miami, and my guy lived in a little house with a big fence running all the way around it. I needed to talk to this guy real quick about something—I forget what—and he wasn't picking up his phone, he's not answering beepers. This guy had, like, fifty kilos of my coke and a couple bales of marijuana in his garage, and he was supposed to move it the next day. Only I had a hair up my ass: I thought something was up with the coke. I wanted to look at it, and this guy wasn't answering his phone. Something's not right."

In hindsight, this is the highlight of my day; not only does Frank give absolutely zero evidence of things not being right, in telling the story it's clear Frank just wanted some of the coke for himself—early in the morning, or very late at night—only his guy won't come to the door to give him some of his own coke. Ergo, proof positive that something's not right . . .

Frank: "Something's not right. We gotta move this stuff the next day. I gotta see what's going on in there. So, fuck it, I'm gonna climb over the fence. Well, I had barely gotten over the top when, bam, a fucking freight train hit me. Bam. It was a Doberman Pinscher, and the scariest thing was the thing didn't make a sound. The dog was completely silent as it tried to rip my windpipe out. I didn't know then that Dobermans never bark. Clearly, I had fucked up jumping the fence. The dog clawed me up awful, but I took one of its eyes, then I got my gun out and put it down. It was a close thing. When he heard the gunshots, my associate came outside, turned some lights on, thought he was gonna shoot me for a minute. I had to go to the hospital. I was pretty bloodied up."

Was your guy mad you'd killed his dog?

Frank: "No, he was just pissed about having to take me to the hospital. And he was like, 'Why the fuck are you trying to get into my yard at 4 a.m.?' We had a good laugh about it. We moved all that coke later that day; it was a good deal. Later on, that guy tried to flip on me. He took some money of mine and ran—but not because I killed his dog.

"We were talking about Mel Fisher, right? He's a famous treasure hunter. I knew Mel in a different way. In my first times bringing in really big shipments I wanted to be there, every step of the way. So, I would go to Key West; that's where things would start. Let me tell you, those trips were not fun. There's only one bridge off the Keys, and it's just not fun. It's scary, it's like driving down a two-lane, dead-end road that they could block at any time, and anything in your ride is gonna be fair game. Then you're down a bunch of cash and the fucking product. The fear of getting popped there was pretty bad. Anyway, the Mel Fisher museum is in Key West. He was a mix—he had boats in the water, so he was trafficking some stuff in addition to the legit treasure hunting business he was doing.

"I first met treasure hunter Mel Fisher in my office. This was 1985. I owned the European Auto Clinic in Virginia Beach right at the foot of the Chesapeake Bay Bridge-Tunnel. We had a double garage with fancy cars coming in and out, and there was a pit sort of thing where you can just drain your motor oil from the lifted cars right into this pit. This is before the EPA. So, there's a grating in the floor and the old oil and gunk just flows into that. So, we would hide the cocaine, guns, and cash in that oil pit, wrapped up in plastic. I had to be far away from the guns because I was a felon.

"So, I'm in my office at European Auto Clinic, and I'm Mister Big at the time. I'm a gangster. You know, it was the '80s. I was an asshole. I'm there one Sunday, and this state trooper comes by and flashes his red and white lights. The state troopers would do that from time to time to fuck with us; make us think, "Uh oh," but really, they're just fucking with us. This state trooper pulled up, we were laughing about the flashing lights, then he says, 'Hey, I got this friend who has a fancy car, and it's fucked up, can you look at it real quick?' I said, 'Hey, it's Sunday, but if it's a friend of yours then no problem.' Try to be friendly with cops if you can in the gangster business—Stanley told me that young.

— Andrew Mallin —

"A tow truck brings in this guy and his car. We were talking as one of the guys in my shop got to work on his car. This guy said, 'Hey man, you're wearing some heavyweight jewelry.' I did, I had some big shit on. So, this guy introduces himself: he's Mel Fisher, and he goes, 'I'm a treasure hunter.' I said, 'Fuck, I'm the same thing.' We liked that.

"Mel had this thing where he'd found some things he did not want to report to the government. I said, 'Hey man'—I'd just come back from India, Indian jewelry is different—I said, 'Don't worry about your car, we'll fix that shit,' and he says, 'Hey, can I show you something?' He wanted to know if I was cool, so I showed him my bookshelf. Press a button and the bookshelf in my office at the auto shop would slide sideways to reveal a little wet bar. I kept some coke and other goodies there. I showed him that, and so he brought out this shit that he already found: chains, rings, doubloons—lot of jewelry, but mostly coins. And I bought a bunch of pieces. I bought one Christ figure of solid gold with emeralds in it. That thing was fucking beautiful. So, I said, 'Mel, I got a guy, Harry Winston. Take my number down. I'll call Harry up, and I'll introduce you. I just want a small percentage.' Because Mel had the goods but didn't know how to move it quietly. Harry Winston had a family business in making this shit go round. I had a relationship with Harry Winston's daughter. So, Mel and I did some deals, then I hooked up Mel and Harry Winston, and I don't know what they all got up to but my little percentage was a nice chunk of dough."

Why were you in the jewelry business?

Frank: "For one thing, the guys who were going back to South America or wherever, they didn't always want cash. If they were going back down there, I might pay them in jewelry. One big ass piece of jewelry is easier to handle than bundles of paper cash.

— Rockstars and Executions —

"Meeting Mel Fisher was right around the time I went to this wedding in India where everyone is riding on elephants, no joke. Me going to the wedding was just an excuse; I hid in India for a year. I worked for Harry Winston [the company] while I was in India. At that time India had all kinds of laws against exporting any culturally significant treasures. So, my job was to help shuffle that in and out of the country, but I had to stay; I was scared to go back to the States to tell you the truth. One deal I did there that went wrong was for a 1912 Rolls-Royce. It had been custom-built for a maharajah. Well, that car never arrived in the USA. I think it's fair to assume someone had tried to move some heroin with the car because that shit was happening all the time. Everything I sent from India, someone would slap some heroin in there. There was too much money to be made not to.

"I was in India when I met Bill Murray. He was in India filming a serious movie. I think it was called *The Darjeeling Limited*? Actually no, that's too recent isn't it? This was sometime around 1985. The *Razor's Edge*, that was it. Bill Murray liked cocaine a little bit, but he really liked to drink, I can tell you that. He was kind of a quiet guy. He and I were staying at the same five-star hotel, and I just said how you doing? He was a little down because he had gotten sick there—you know, stomach—so I said, 'Shit, I got a little sick too.' I actually had malaria, if I remember. So yeah, he was a little bit down. I saw him again later by the pool and we talked a little bit, but he wasn't no laugh-a-minute kind of guy. He was a pretty serious and quiet guy; that surprised me. We ended up hanging by the pool for a couple hours having drinks—was the only thing that could make you feel better. I told Bill I had been offered a tour with Eddie Murphy, but I had to turn it down because I was making too much money with my cocaine business. Bill said I could have taken my cocaine business on the road with Eddie.

"If there was anyone I could've gone on the road with, that I would've wanted to see play every night, it would've been Jerry Lee Lewis.

"I was working the Volunteer Jam with Billy Joel's bodyguard, Bill Snouffer, and Billy Joel calls up Bill and says, 'I'm coming down.' Billy Joel lives in New York. So, he flies down, and we're walking around early in the day; it was light out, and nobody recognized Billy Joel. The fucker is at the height of his fame, but this ain't his crowd. And we're walking around tooting coke, and Billy Joel felt a little out of place because he's not country, but we're having a good time. Bill and I are doing security, but it was pretty laidback that early in the day, so we just strolled around. The Volunteer Jam venue is huge, there are little stages all over the place for little acts. So, we're walking around, and there's all these different stages, and one of them is this little-ass stage with a piano on it. Billy goes, 'I'll play something.' He could play anything. So, Billy Joel asks me what's my favorite band. I said, 'Hey man, I love Jerry Lee Lewis.' Well, within about five minutes Billy Joel is doing the whole thing: he's playing the piano with his feet, he's doing the whole Jerry Lee Lewis. And people are swarming over to us. He was pounding that piano, hammering on the keys. Nobody there really knew he was famous as hell, nobody cared, he was just as good as Jerry Lee Lewis. Now, everyone thought he was dressed like an asshole—he wasn't dressed country—and me and Bill Snouffer are two tough guys in black shirts, so we blended in alright. Billy Joel, kicking feet up on the piano. He was great. He brought the fucking house down. I remember famous acts were coming up to me the rest of that Jam, saying, you see that crazy fucker on the piano? That fucker could play! It was

— Rockstars and Executions —

Billy Joel.

"Little Richard and Jerry Lee Lewis got along. They were good friends, I think, and man, they could play. They would put on a show. The only other act that cool was Chuck Berry. Chuck did the thing with his guitar that the guys from AC/DC copied—where he's playing and they kinda walk up along the instrument, you know?"

My notes from that evening: Frank has taken to calling the room where we do these interviews The Confessional. The bit of the story where he went to the sports store and bought a bat because it was a subdivision and he couldn't be loud when he killed Gilbert's wife, that scared me. I did not enjoy being in the room in that moment. I'm quite the scaredy-cat. He's quite possibly a monster.

But the thing with Mel Fisher was just plain weird.

I was walking in this morning with my coffee and laptop bag, and as he was opening the door to The Confessional he said, "You want to talk about Mel Fisher?" I said, "What?" He said it again, "Mel Fisher." I said, "The treasure hunter?" Frank said, "Yeah."

I had never heard the name Mel Fisher until the previous night. I was noodling around Wikipedia, crushing some "On This Day" content, and I stumbled onto the Mel Fisher wiki page. I read about the accident with his family that happened right before he hit it big, and I had thought that's a good fiction story if you flip the narrative and the fictional Mel actually clipped his wife and partner. Maybe they were bangin' behind his back, and his son happened to be aboard the day the fictional Mel got his revenge. The fictional Mel taking out his own son as unintended collateral damage. I was thinking how a fictional character like that might be destroyed by guilt but would likely eke out an existence, would cling to life even in

— 76 —

deepest despair. Basically, I thought he'd make a great bad guy for a story. And today, out of nowhere, Frank is telling me that Mel Fisher had treasure out the wazoo before he hit it big officially. I don't feel comfortable publishing what Frank has said about Mel as fact. It's just wild that he played into a fiction that I had in my head. Just a coincidence, nothing more. . . . right?

Day Five

Kathleen

Warm rain hammers at the windows. Kitty is tired; she has climbed the stairs to the second floor. Before she walks into The Confessional, Frank asks her, "How you feeling? You feeling good?" He grabs my arm, pulls me back out of the room, tells me to keep it under five minutes with her today. She's tired, and he wants to try for the beach with her later today.

Kathleen: "Me arriving at Yale was a bit like a fish going to the moon. I was invited there two weeks early along with the other honors poor kids. We learned what it would be like to be in a residential school. It was a great program to help us get up to speed. And so I met a couple people there in orientation that became friends for life. School started and I felt intimidated as hell; the kids from private school just had such a leg up. That semester I got my first B, a B-plus. My English professor said, 'I'm going to give you this extra work'—after one semester I felt caught up. The best part of the experience was the professor mentoring me, she took me out to coffee and she said you're just as smart as any of these kids, you just need to catch up. And I started sobbing. After that though, I really enjoyed my first year. For the first time ever I had friends that were my caliber, you know? They read books and stuff.

"That summer I went home and worked at the Stone Mountain water park. The water park was up on some hills, and we had these silly little rides you'd slide down, and I'd be up top of the slide, and if there were any accidents I'd have to run along the side and help the kids out. I had a ball. I just loved hanging with the little kids too. I got my little brother hired so he was there too; that was fun. The mountain was five miles around, so I would run around it every day. I was very thin, but in good shape, which felt really good, you know?

"When I was a junior, I became chairman of the Yale Charities Drive. We used this money to assist disadvantaged people in New Haven. I was elected to something called 'secret society'—there's one called 'Skull and Bones' or 'Omicron Chi,' but the one I was a member of was 'Stone and Snake.' You'd meet twice a week and learn about each other's personal history. People were wonderful to be around. They learned I came from a dirt-poor background, and they would take me to lakes and stuff, we all hung around. I was a straight-A student senior year, runner-up for the Rhodes Scholarship and graduated magna cum laude. The person who won the Rhodes Scholarship deserved it.

"When I think about Yale, I think about Bart Giamatti. He was friendly and helpful. He wanted to help, but he said, 'Kitty, this is Yale. People don't do charities, they don't like giving away money.' I said, 'Well, we'll have parties then. Everyone likes to party, and we'll get them to give to charity while they're busy having fun.' Bart was very supportive. I think it was his letter of recommendation that got me into Columbia. He also nominated me for the Yale Senior Scholarship award."

— Andrew Mallin —

*****

Frank

"I went to the gym this morning at 12:30 a.m. I go every morning. I'll tell you a secret: I put pen to paper—I don't write it on a computer or a phone—I put pen to paper on what I'm going to do the next day. Right before bed, think about the day you want to have tomorrow, and the things you write down will be yours to do. I do *kaya sthairyam* throughout the day—that's a type of meditation."

He runs to his room and returns with a handwritten book: *Pranayama, the Art and Science of Energy Guidance.*

"I put this book together. I would teach other people from this book. Now, helping people whose energy has gone is what I do now. That's what I'm doing with Kitty. That is how I'm bringing her back from the grave. She's not my first though. I started this when I was still a rock and roll security guy and a gangster. I was visiting New Orleans, and a friend of a friend was this guy who produced the movies *Secretariat* and *Iron Man* among others. He hired me to work with his wife; she was an alcoholic, and she had got into a car wreck. She was in a bad way. I stayed with that wife of his right there on Lincoln Court for almost half a year, and I got paid real well to help get her straight. That experience kind of clued me in on what I should do after being a gangster."

When did you stop being a drug dealer, gangster, whatever?

Frank: "For me, it would've stopped . . . well, I didn't entirely stop because I would start again when I needed cash. The first run was 1971 to 1983, I can tell you that. I pretty much lost everything I had to US Customs because of a plane and a boat. The plane was a Cessna that we were flying in and out of a clearing outside Bolivia, North Carolina. There's a bunch of big farms there that an associate owned. There was the big swamp behind us, it was right over Cape Fear—it was a primo spot. One time, I wasn't there, and for some reason the county truck wasn't either. See, we usually used these county government trucks—you know, public works department?—because it's a state forest near there and they blend in and I had a friend who could get one. Well, for whatever reason, the county truck didn't show, so my guy took his wife's car. It was this little two-door rig, and it was not the car for this job. This plane carried bales of marijuana. These things take up a lot of space. What was he thinking he'd do, strap 'em to the fucking hood? I never got to ask him, not that I would've wanted to know what he had to say. Well, the plane lands, they unload it, and the plane takes off with my guy talking about making a couple trips. Instead, he probably figures one trip is less risk than two. Now, I saw pictures afterwards. No joke, this fucking asshole had bales of weed tied to the top of his car. He did not have room to turn really as he drove (because) there were so many bales of weed in the passenger seat. He'd tied his trunk down, bales of weed poking up out of it. His wife's stupid little Pinto was fucking bursting with weed. He was supposed to drive to Myrtle Beach. We're talking, like, forty-five miles here; this is not a ride down the block. I don't know what he was thinking. He didn't even make it to the South Carolina border because, get this, he took a blind right turn because he couldn't see around the weed, and he side-swiped a road sign in front of a sheriff. He told them everything: that one plane was just me, none of my associates. I think they got some of our guys in the Bahamas too because of the plane. All of that one fell pretty squarely on me. The problem was the shrimping boat had just gotten picked up too, so that was that.

"The shrimp boat operated out of Fort Lauderdale, Florida, and it was a pretty sweet operation. It would go out and pick out packages dropped from a plane that flew out of the Bahamas. I'm pretty sure it was a DC-4, one of them big, four-propeller planes from World War Two. Some associates had bought it and taken all the seats out of the plane. They would load up this thing like a pallet size and push a couple of them out the door as it flew over a course the shrimping boat knew to follow. They would lose a fair amount of these packages—the ocean is the ocean—but it was a nifty way to do things. We would let them dry. Sometimes, if we were in a hurry, we'd take hairdryers to the plastic packaging so we could cut 'em open quicker. When the Miami Airport connection closed down, and that one at the airport was the big one for a lot of people, we tried a couple things. We tried a connection in Houston, but it wasn't good for us. Through the Colombians we got introduced to this guy, John Q, a couple years back. His father and brother had been Green Berets, and (when) he went into gangsterland, he was not exactly someone to pick a fight with. I kept it cool around him. I worked out of Miami and Virginia Beach, and this guy, John Q, was doing stuff in Texas. He was dealing with some heavy duty tattooed Mexicans. These guys didn't belong in Virginia Beach. He brought them up once right after we all met, and I had more heat on me that fucking weekend than I ever did before or after. We couldn't get fifty feet from my shop without getting pulled over. Anyway, Houston was going to be a new connection; it was going to be the connection for the coke. This guy, John Q—I saw a picture of his brother, who was in El Salvador with the Green Berets, they were doing some gruesome shit down there. John Q was a straight-up guy, but look, people disappeared in Houston who were on that deal. I don't really know what happened, just that the guys who were supposed to be working with us were from Guadalajara because that's where their associates were from, you know? See, once whatever had happened with John Q and the Mexicans, the Mexicans had other guys come up because when word got around he had disappeared their crew, the shit hit the fan. John Q was a big guy; he could fight. I was in his car once, and he had hand grenades in the glove box. No shit, he had a couple of them in there right on top of some bandannas. He was ready. Well, John Q disappeared, and the guys from Guadalajara made it clear Houston was not going to work for the out-of-towners who had been working with John Q.

"So that's why we had a couple groups who were interested in putting together what it took to get the shrimp boat thing off the ground. It's not always easy to find guys who can work a ship and be trusted not to get drunk and talk about it. Pilots were always hard to come by. We paid for a couple guys to get their pilot licenses, and one of them just fucked off. I think they found him in the Philippines, and the others were all drunks. So, keeping the shrimping boat going wasn't easy, but we brought in, shit, a couple thousand kilos over the years we had it. And how do you think it got fucked up? Two guys and one girl, of course. One guy we were working with was fucking another guy's girlfriend, and so the guy killed the guy who was fucking his girlfriend—only the girlfriend tells the cops her boyfriend's been murdered, and she knows who did it, and what boat to find him on. Well, there was a lot of shit on that shrimp boat. A lot of people flipped on me right there in '83.

"Here's the thing about when did I stop being a gangster. I got cleaned out once, and then I got done again a bit worse, but I could go back and forth with you all day as to what the answer is. People still bug me because they needed connections and they need introductions, and so it never really stops.

"I can say I was allowed to travel after my first bust. Do not write the word *cooperated*. I called my son, my oldest, and said, 'I'm gonna get lost for a while.' I was up against it, and there were three guys who did me—they fucked up first, and I'm gonna kill these motherfuckers. It's the middle of the day. I'm trying to talk myself into it. I have to disown my family. If I can get this bunch of money I don't need to worry about coming and getting them, they would be able to come to me in their time. I'm making my plans while I'm sitting at the table. I don't know, it was some fucking crazy stupid plans. And I look up because there's someone else in the room all of a sudden—and I was not drinking, I was not doing drugs—and then all of a sudden, there was three little angelic things in the corner. And then a voice came into my ears and said, 'Everything is going to be okay Frankie.' It was my Uncle Stanley's voice. And I put my head down on the table, and I knew I wasn't going to kill them. I didn't want to die making mistakes. One of my sons was born that year. His mom was an ER nurse. I didn't meet him 'til he was a couple years old.

"When I was in India my old partner stole a hundred grand from my wife. I was in India for a year—well, it was Kashmir for a while; that's sort of different from India. I wasn't allowed back in the country, and he was supposed to turn in a couple titled cars—they were legit—and give the cash to my wife. Well, he took the cars, and he had his wife go over there to my house and tell my wife this fucking sob story about needing the money to buy a stake in a new jewelry store. Her husband had the experience to start a new one, so on and so on. They took off. I smoked some opium in India. Everyone was doing it; it was almost as popular as the marijuana there. I worked on my spirit. I found myself there. I don't know if I ever stopped anything, but that's where I stopped carrying a gun. Friends had helped get me to Kashmir, so I needed to get out of there, I needed my spirit to be new, you know? So, I went to Kathmandu. That's Nepal. It's a huge city; it was good to start new there. I came back to the States clean."

The phone began ringing sometime after Kashmir but before Kathmandu.

Billy Vans (name changed): "Frank, you fucking nutjob, what's up you crazy son of a bitch?"

Frank: "Hey Billy, I'm here with that writer man I told you about. I want to talk about the drugs you got arrested for on the shrimp boat, but hey, I'm not gonna tell him about the fat guy."

Billy: "Yeah, that's a good idea. Hey, writer man. By the way, you know he's dead right?"

Frank: "He's dead?"

Billy: "Yeah man, the fat man has gone."

Frank: "Well, fuck it then. We can talk about the fat man. Billy, tell him how long you were in jail for."

Billy: "I did eight years in the pen. When we got caught on the shrimp boat they tried to say I was in a leadership role, that I ran one cell of the cartel. They said all kinds of shit, but I just kept it shut. They took my cash, they took the house I had my girlfriend buy, they took my boats, they took my jet skis, and they gave me eight years. They got me on the Interstate. I was headed to Miami, and I had just got off the boat. I remember I was talking to your son on the car phone when I got pulled over. I told your kid they might be putting me in jail. They never had me in possession—not a gram, nothing. But I had a couple weapons on me, and they were able to make the charges stick."

Frank: "Hey Billy, you remember the first time you met me, when you started working for me?"

Billy: "Actually, I do. I must've been twelve and you came to visit my grandma's. You gave me a hundred and fifty bucks, a lot of money for back then. And you were like, 'Go buy scratch-off lotto tickets, exactly one and fifty dollars' worth.' So, I went to the corner score with a big wad of money, and I must've bought a couple hundred scratch-offs, and I bring them back to my grandma's, and you tell me to scratch 'em off and I'll be able to keep half of whatever we win. Well, I remember this for two reasons. The first is I didn't win jack shit. The second is, you realize how much of that grey scratch-off stuff is on a hundred and fifty bucks worth of scratch-offs? My grandmother gave me grief for the next decade over that I think. That stuff was all over her house."

Frank: "Oh shit, I forgot that was your grandma's house."

Billy: "Yeah. And I started working for you at the car place, whatever it was called, European Car Clinic."

Frank: "What'd you do working for me?"

Billy: "Well, mostly you had me working on that bookshelf of yours. That thing worked about one day a year. And you had me driving drugs up and down the East Coast."

Frank: "But about the shrimp boat."

Billy: "Oh yeah. I would meet the boat at the dock. There was a little building there on the dock that you could drive straight into. I would meet the guys there."

Frank: "Do you remember what happened in Houston before we did the shrimp boat?"

— Rockstars and Executions —

Billy: "I remember what happened after Houston! Shit, Frank, you know I wasn't in Houston. But yeah, I went to Guadalajara after that to try and, you know, I mean, like you always said they knew we were good about money, we ran a good crew. Is the writer man really gonna write all this down?"

Me: "I don't have t---"

Frank: "He's writing it down, yeah. It's time to rock and roll, got to tell the story man. Go on brother."

Billy: "I was in Guadalajara, I had four guys we had arranged to carry the money. They were with another group of guys, and they were kinda brokering what we had to do, which was to say, 'We're real sorry about all that happened, and here's a shitload of money, can we have drugs now please?' As you can tell, I don't really give a shit anymore. Frank can vouch for that."

Frank: "Billy will fuck you up. He got fucking huge in prison. He's still big, but holy shit I saw a picture of him the day he got of jail. He sent it to me, and my man was fucking bigger than hell."

Billy: "Nothing else to do in there, right?"

Frank: "Yeah man, that's good. Go on."

Billy: "So I'm with the four guys who I flew there with, and we have the cash in briefcases and these two duffel bags. We were in a boot place, a boot store. We're sitting around in the chairs, there was music playing, we were drinking these small little beers they only have in Mexico. These things were tiny, like two tips of the can and it's empty. It's not really the point, but come to think of it, those things are weird. I'm in the boot shop, and I'm the only gringo there, and my four guys just fucking vanish like smoke. They flew out the front door. In the back door came six guys. They put me in a hood. There's a real big church in Guadalajara—it's impressive, worth checking out if you can. I had gone to church that morning, and I remember the moment after the hood went over my head thinking how glad I was that I'd been to church that day. Shit, Frankie."

Frank: "They were pissed."

Billly: "I'll say. They drove me out of town. We were in a big white limo. They beat me up pretty bad, said the payment for the misunderstanding was good and fine and to basically fuck off, no drugs. It wasn't that bad. But, you know, I remember it from time to time. It wasn't the most fun I've ever had."

Frank: "Tell him about DC. Tell him about DC."

Billy: "I got a phone call I never like. It's Frank saying come up to DC real fucking quick. This was middle of the night. He gives me an address. He sounded pretty tight. This was maybe a month after I got back from Mexico."

Frank: "These were the guys—well, they were kinda the main guys in Mexico then. When they called me after Billy got back to tell me we gotta meet, I thought that was it, we were getting called there to get killed. I went solo. I told Billy to be ready to run for the fucking hills if he didn't hear from me."

Billy: "Now, like I told you, I worked at Frank's auto clinic. We have those huge scales that you can drive the cars onto and weigh them, right? So, I had some experience fixing those things. I get the call in the middle of the night to drive from Virginia Beach up to DC. The whole time I'm driving up I'm thinking, 'This is probably it.' I get to the address and it's a warehouse. Well, shit, I think I might've called my girlfriend and said bye real quick."

Frank: "Did you really?"

Billy: "Yeah man, you weren't in Mexico. I thought that was it. So, I walk in and this warehouse is pitch black, dark as night, only I can hear a bunch of talking, and I'm just expecting them to empty into me at any moment. Well, it's a bunch of them standing around with Frank, and they lead me into the next building over. Frank had given me the wrong address and had the guys come over there to bring me to the right place."

Frank: "I got the street number wrong, and you weren't picking up on your way up."

Billy: "So we go into the next building and there is a bunch of the baddest dudes of all time standing around looking like a bunch of lost schoolchildren, standing around a van that had got stuck atop a car lift. They looked like such a bunch of fucking idiots."

Frank: "They knew I weighed the bales on my car lifts, and they just wanted us to fix that thing so they could get their shit down and get the fuck out of there. It had nothing to do with Houston."

Billy: "I tell you that drive back to Virginia Beach was the best four hours of my life."

Frank: "Tell him about the polygraph."

Billy: "They flew this lady in from California. They had me in the federal building in Norfolk, and they put me on a polygraph. I asked what the deal was, and they said if I fail this thing then I'm looking at more charges. Well, I failed when they ask me my name. It's my name. The thing said I'm lying. I said, 'How can you trust this piece of shit?'"

Frank: "Alright Billy, you be good man. I'll talk to you soon."

Billy: "Hey man, you be good. Good talking to you."

Frank: "Of all the rock and roll acts I saw do the thing, I think the one guy who was most ahead of his time was Prince. He was no throwback. He was no Michael Jackson. He was everything. He was a mix of everything. Michael Jackson was one hell of a dancer, but he couldn't really sing. I mean, he had some good songs, but you know that's a lot of production. I think the most intelligent guy was Prince or Billy Joel. Prince was the whole everything. He could get up on stage and have the place hanging on him—like every time he blinked it was a big deal—and he also wrote songs that had some meaning. Yeah, Prince was ahead of his time. But, okay, I worked a Prince tour. Who else was ahead of their time? The first is Little Richard. And I'm not saying this, but the other one is James Brown. That's just from talking to people who know; people who know talk about James Brown. I only got to see him once, but everyone who knows said James Brown was one of the greatest ever at all of it. All of it. And then the third is Jerry Lee Lewis. He knew it was short time, short time you get with a crowd, and he worked it.

"Was I spiritual before India? I wasn't spiritual yet, no, but I had that Catholic imprint. I had that religious imprint. That stuff is always with me. It was always with me. But no, I was not spiritual then when I had a bunch of hard-ass gangsters work for me. I had my religion. It was in the back of my mind. But no, I was not spiritual yet. I remember I was with the Oak Ridge Boys, and they sing gospel songs on stage, and I'm on the bus with them, and they are snorting all the cocaine. That was my first 'hmm' moment about spirituality. Those songs were just words to those boys; they didn't meet shit.

"The least spiritual guy I ever met? I know who that was: Rick fucking James. He's a freak—you should believe him when he tells you he's a freak. I heard that Rick James had a thing for tying up women, and I don't mean in bed having fun. Tying up women and leaving them. People who worked security for Rick James knew to look in the trunk of Rick James' limo because half the time he'd have tied some woman up in there. He was a mean motherfucker when he was on drugs, and he was always on drugs. But he was a star, so you can get away with it.

"Growing up in the rock and roll industry, black people tended to go to black acts and white people to white bands. The first big crossover band was The Commodores. They appealed to everyone. Everyone liked them. The Commodores were one of the first tours I did part of. I did a couple states with them, a show a night. I'll never forget Lionel Richie asking for the polio pot. I asked him what that was. He said, 'It's that pot that makes you seize up.' Lionel Richie got pulled over when he was driving one of the limos in Texas. They had just got back from Martha's Vineyard, up near Boston, and they'd been harassed pretty good up there. Well, this Texas Ranger asked what an N---- was doing driving this limo. If he knew the Commodores were big he didn't seem to care. He found a couple joints in the limo and things were going to be bad there for a minute. Then their manager said all the joints were his and the limo was in his name. I think he did a couple months in a Texas jail. That was one of my very first times touring with an act. Lionel Richie and the Commodores, they were good guys. It was a good tour."

Did your father ever try to dissuade you from your lifestyle?

Frank: "Okay, my father had a small safe in his office at my parents' house, and soon after I got my '69 GTO I said, 'Dad, can I use your safe?' He said, 'Yeah, you can use it.' I said, 'Thanks, can you take your stuff out and put it someplace else?' I said, 'Don't ask a whole load of questions.' I said, 'I'm going to fill this safe up.' He said, 'What you gonna fill it with?'

I said, 'I'm gonna fill it with hundred-dollar bills.' And a couple months later, I had a huge smile on my face. I showed him how his little old safe was full. I asked him to do me a favor, and he went to Tweeds Locksmith in Portsmouth, Virginia, and he got the biggest safe he could find.

"He didn't know what I was doing, but he knew. You know what I mean? He didn't know anything about cocaine, but he knew what else I was doing. The story I can tell you about my dad, though, is I was down in Miami with the Cubans and they're asking me, 'We'll take a tractor trailer from Miami to New York.' I didn't want my father to get caught, though. I told the Cubans, 'This what we're gonna do: we'll fill that thing up and drive it up to New York, and bam, you've just tripled the price of the stuff in the truck. It's worth triple in New York what it's worth in Miami. So, you're seeing what I'm saying: we'll put the drugs in the center, and we'll layer oranges all around the drugs.' So, I said, 'I'm not using my fucking father to be in that truck.' I said, 'I want a Cuban driver.' My dad was supposed to drive this truck, and he wasn't gonna know what was packed in back. Shit was fucked up. So, I took my father, and I put him in a hotel room. I hid him from the Cubans. I said, 'Go to a restaurant, hang out, do whatever the fuck you want, just lay low. 'And I stayed ready because what I did was stood ready, and if the truck got pinched or anything happened on the trip to New York, I was there ready to drop a dime and say this truck has got stolen, and I would tie up my father and make it look like he got abducted and his truck stolen. But the truck got through to Miami with the Cuban driving, no problems. I felt like shit after that, I said no more involving my father.

"The best way to carry ten to twenty kilos is in the spare tire of eighteen-wheelers. Back then there were not as many drug-sniffing dogs as they have now. Fish trucks were just as big as regular eighteen-wheelers. The fish go in the middle with ice all around them. It stunk to fucking hell, but the keys of coke would go right there in the middle in plastic and nobody would want to dig into it.

"All of this happened after the Miami airport connection went dead. See, at the Miami airport there was a Goodyear garage and gas station right there next to the back gate of the airport. The guys who worked the back gate were all connected and taking money from people like me. We would try to do this on Saturday or Sunday mornings or Monday nights, never during the week. We would drive into a bay of that Goodyear garage. Without (us) getting out of the van, they'd open the van doors and they would throw the shit into the vans. Now, we still had to weigh the shit, so what we would do is drive the vans onto mechanical lifts. We have weight sensors on those things, so we'd make sure the weight looked good right there on the jack. *Monday Night Football* was the absolute best time to move weight. The Dolphins weren't that bad for a while, and all the cops would act busy when they were playing on Monday nights.

"The highest energy concert I ever worked was AC/DC. It was pandemonium. It was kinda like just strap in and hold on for a couple hours. There were some brick shithouses at that show, and they were all taking swings they were so keyed up. I remember I stayed at the venue and did breathing exercises for a couple hours after their show that night. I had a couple dust ups, and I wanted to settle down. You asked me when did I discover yoga? Well, I was only fourteen years old when I saw yoga being practiced on a Skippy Peanut Butter Hour—you know, on TV?" Skippy Peanut Butter Hour?

"Yeah, there was a tv show—this was many years ago—they would do an hour on all kinds of different or, you know, new things. I don't know how to explain it, but I remember the name Skippy Peanut Butter, so I guess it did its job. I saw yoga on that show, then I took a book out of the Portsmouth library. This was when I was just starting to get into boxing and I was playing football pretty seriously in high school. I wanted to be a football player for a long time. After I found that book at the library I started working that stuff into my training. I started building my breath. So, when I was in Kashmir and Kathmandu, you know, I had an appreciation for what I was being shown, you know?

"You asked if I carried anything like brass knuckles when I was working security for rock and roll shows? Yeah, there were guys with things like that, but I preferred a fork."

A fork? Frank leaves the room and returns with a regular four-tined fork in his hand. It disappears up his sleeve.

"Do you know what happens when you fuck with the face, when it gets cut?"

You bleed a lot?

"Fucking-A right. Even without that bad of a wound, your face will bleed like crazy. You can break bones to put someone down, but someone that is bleeding isn't fighting. If you've got blood in your eyes, you stop caring about other shit. I wasn't supposed to have a gun at the venue, and I didn't want a knife. I had a fork."

He demonstrates how he'd rake my forehead with the fork, the fork out and gone in a flash. I don't know if it's impressively simple, or I'm back in second grade and Michael Owens is swearing his dad is a professional ninja, because Mike owns a plastic ninja throwing star.

About five times today Frank has talked about heroin and about how he never ever moved it or touched the stuff. But each time he mentions it, it's because he's talking about moving it in deals. So, I'd say he's keeping that bit of his past under wraps. It's also a pattern with Frank though, a mannerism almost: he'll say something, like he can't remember where he saw James Brown live, then five minutes later he's talking about doing security at a James Brown show. His memories eddy and chase one another.

It struck me funny tonight, recounting Frank talking about these deep spiritual thoughts, these deep breathing exercises, these calming gentle practices of serenity . . . and every now and again he interrupts this serenity to holler as loudly as possible for Kitty's dog to get off the damn couch or stop fucking barking.

Right before I left for the day, Frank grabbed his iPad and showed me a movie trailer. He was very excited to show me this thing. His iPad has a video saved on it. He's recorded another device playing the YouTube video. Name of video: "*John Jumano* Trailer." View count: 325. Comments: Two.

Tonight I went back and watched the trailer again, and sweet mother mercy, it did not disappoint. It is completely unhinged. Pretty fucking violent. The comments slayed me. User Nate Diggity opined, "It's a real shame only 173 people have seen this. Jack Charles is the real deal." Well, Nate, almost twice as many people have seen it now, rest in strength. And who the hell is Jack Charles? The second comment, though, is where the real gold is. This is someone who is either an undercover cop on a fishing expedition or it's someone the FBI really ought to take a close look at. User A GG had this to say: "Hi, longtime admirer, first time commenter. Can you answer the following question, please? It would really make this fan's

Andrew Mallin

day! Is this movie based on real-life events?" In the trailer, Frank shoots two women point blank while a child (age: three to five-ish) cowers in the corner. Note to self: avoid YouTube user A GG in real life.

Day Six

Kathleen

"When Roger Coleman was on death row, I had experienced executions from afar through my work at NAACP Legal Defense Fund in law school, but I hadn't been close. Roger got better treatment on death row than he would've gotten in gen pop; that's just one of the oddities of our penal system. Roger was writing personal letters directly to the Attorney General of Virginia, the person in charge of making sure his execution went through. They let Roger go from death row to maximum security to educate others. He would go to the guys in maximum security and talk to them about how to self-educate, how to get GEDs and apply for parole, things like that—which was kinda wild because he was coming from death row with that message. When Roger was executed they had a civilian take over that educational position. It was interesting to him that Roger was so productive on death row given that in normal life he would've been just a coal miner. That's what Roger was, a coal miner. On death row, he was writing and reading, he had an interest in foreign affairs. I arranged to have a prison psychologist come in to try and determine Roger's innocence because I had a point where I had to step back and ask myself, 'Am I just being dumb here? Am I being fooled?' I hired a bastard of a psychologist. This guy is tough. He and Roger went through Roger's life and did two eight-hour sessions, and (at) the end of that the psychologist didn't like Roger much, but he said Roger was being honest about his innocence.

"I was a voting Republican at the time, but I always (was) accused of being Miss Liberal. It was tough going on shows like *Nightline* to talk about the innocence cases and the penal system in this country because I was a pretty young woman, and I get it, they would think I'm an idiot for believing a liar and murderer. I do believe in execution as a deterrent against specific crimes, but broadly I do not believe in the justice of our system of incarceration or execution that we have in this country."

Were you on *Nightline*?

"I was on all the shows trying to get Roger's innocence some attention. If you look up my name and Roger Keith Coleman, you should find them."

Why do they do that with middle names? I'm Andrew Mallin, but if I killed someone would everyone address me as Andrew William Mallin?

(laughs) "I said to Roger, I never would've known your middle name if you weren't on death row.

"Roger's execution was terribly rough. I was there with Jim McCloskey. Jim is a private investigator who had volunteered his time after Roger wrote to him. Jim was working the case long before we were there. Jim has a company, Centurion Ministries; they still exist, helping people on death row.

"Around the time of the execution I was getting death threats, so the law firm said I could go but only at my own risk. I wasn't allowed to bring any of the other lawyers who had tried to help Roger. So it was really just me and Jim. We were with Roger that night in the cell. They had taken two cells and combined them into one big one. It was really quite grim as you can imagine. They had Roger get undressed, they shaved his head, and then Roger said 'I hope someday Virginia will recognize that I was innocent, and they will re-evaluate their need for the death penalty in this country.' Then Jim and I waited in the waiting room as they electrocuted him. And it burned his head and his skin, and everything was pretty awful. I took the first and longest vacation of my career. Two weeks. After that, I said I'm not taking another case of an innocent man on death row. I couldn't do it.

Then six months later, I started working pro bono for Troy Anthony Davis."

Did you like Marc Rich?

"I did. He was very personable, but I liked him because you could ask him the dirtiest dirt questions and he would answer quick and to the point. Pincus was one for ten-minute answers that didn't answer anything. Marc just answered. I even asked him, 'Are you working for someone at the CIA?' We had heard the rumor. He answered that he could connect with people in Israel that someone from the government couldn't so I'm going to help my country. Even as the federal government was prosecuting him, Marc was working for the CIA. I visited him in Switzerland; it was a long flight back. When I landed I called him outside our group calls. I said, 'Marc, why do you need this pardon?' He could've done a lot of other things with his money and influence. Let's not kid ourselves, a guy with money like Marc's has influence. He wanted the pardon because he felt he was innocent. The pardon petition we wrote is out there, so you can look it up and find my reasons for agreeing that he was innocent."

Where did Marc Rich live then? "He had houses in Spain, Switzer land, Portugal, and Israel. He traveled with a number of big bodyguards."

*****

Frank

"I did security for Crosby, Stills, Nash & Young at Foreman Field, Norfolk, Virginia. They played for three hours. They did not need an opener. It was sunny and hot as shit. I remember David Crosby liked that my arms were fucking huge. David Crosby liked to poke me in the arm, I'd make a muscle, and he'd have a laugh. It was so fucking hot that day that even the band members were getting a little sick. Stephen Stills and them were really just regular guys at the time; they couldn't have been nicer. I did shows with Neil Young afterwards. He went solo, in case you didn't hear. Kind of a peculiar guy but alright. Kind of rough cut. Not a dancer or a mover, you know what I mean? Neil Young was more inward than most. He had a real distinct voice ,and I think that kind of silver voice comes from within.

"The Doobie Brothers are good guys. Michael McDonald was real good to everyone on the road. He was respectful and thoughtful—they all were. That was a very good band of people. After the thing (rock show) they liked to party. They all liked the coke and the booze. It was just a fun time with them every time. Bill Snouffer and I loved working Doobie Brothers shows. Bill did a couple tours with them.

"Different venues are (like) different human beings. The ones in Norfolk are home territory for me. Sure there's rough people, but it's no big deal. But when it got to Richmond, you'd get more bikers there, and the more bikers at a show, they can be annoying. Just a lot more fights. They like to hang in big groups because most of them cannot fight for shit. But a big group of bikers get together it's almost a guaranteed fight. And if they're doing that crystal meth, well, then any one of 'em can fight. (laughs)

"The Doobie Brothers loved this bar. It was called the Golden Triangle, and it was right next to The Scope. The Scope is the venue in Norfolk, Virginia. The bar was right next door, and the band The Doobie Brothers closed that bar down a few times.

"The Oak Ridge Boys and Roy Orbison were performing at The Scope in Norfolk. I made sure they got in their hotel rooms alright because it was snowing. We had a couple delays, but whatever, we were rock and rolling. Roy Orbison was supposed to go on first, but Roy had slipped coming off the bus. His eyesight was not great, and his health was never very good anyway. So they had a block of rooms in this hotel, and we're getting ready to go to sound check, and—I didn't find this out 'til later after sound check—they went back to the hotel to relax and someone has given Roy Orbison a shitload of painkillers, and now Roy Orbison is missing. And the Oak Ridge Boys were pissed. It was snowing like a motherfucker, but I ran back to the fucking hotel. I kicked in Roy Orbison's door because the manager wouldn't open it for me. I said, 'Roy, you gotta get going, man. You're running fucking late, man.' Roy had an assistant. That guy made sure Roy's hair was alright; that felt like the priority even though we were running late. We were all three of us all in black. Roy Orbison's assistant brought out a fucking baby bottle. It was a baby bottle. Full of honey, soda water and maybe something else.

"Roy Orbison is very sensitive to light. That's why he wears them glasses. So we were about to go on stage finally and Roy Orbison was

— Rockstars and Executions —

looking a little skittish, but he played the show and he played fucking perfectly, every note. Roy finishes, and so he leaves while I'm there working the Oak Ridge Boys. They sing their gospel. I'm getting everyone on the bus after the show, and I haven't seen Roy in a couple hours, but that's fine. They had a couple hours after the show. So it was me, Steve Gudis, and the Oak Ridge Boys doing coke, and we're having fun, and Roy Orbison hadn't been around in a few hours. So then the Oak Ridge Boys were all shitting on Roy Orbison. They were talking about him, like, you know, like he's fucking holding them back. I wish Steve Gudis was still alive. I'd call him right now. Holy shit, I forgot about this. I said, "Do you think everyone there tonight came to see you guys?" I was explaining to the Oak Ridge Boys—and these guys were fucking famous too—Roy Orbison fucking slipped and got hurt; he put on a great show. I bet you half of that crowd tonight was there to see him. I said he's a fucking legend. I said, 'Yeah, he fell and he was on drugs, but he can sing.' And they were kinda cool about it, and Steve was there, and Steve is a funny guy. He made it smooth. But they were kinda hush after that. That was not the only show I did with Roy Orbison. If you listen to his songs, he was just like a notch, maybe two notches, below Elvis Presley when Elvis had the best singing voice in the world. That's how good Roy was. He was a legend, and I told Steve Gudis and the Oak Ridge Boys to show him some respect. Steve had been already, of course, I was just talking to the room."

Stephen Gudis has passed, but the famous promoter John Campbell (name changed) is very much alive.

"John, who were your three favorite bands from when I was working rock and roll?"

John: "Oh, that's a tough one. Charlie Daniels is top of the list because him and everyone around him were great guys. Charlie always took care of us at the Volunteer Jam. The same guys who were working for Charlie Daniels when he came up in the '70s were the same guys who were working for Charlie when he died two years ago. That should tell you everything you need to know about Charlie Daniels. He was a great guy. Nothing crazy, he was just a normal guy, he was a personable, caring guy.

"Poco?"

Poco? I've never heard of them.

"Yeah, Poco (is) number two. Two of the guys were from Buffalo Springfield, and two of the guys were in The Eagles. Their lineup changed a lot, but the guys in Poco were all good people.

"Aerosmith. I liked them a lot, but they were difficult. It wasn't their attitude that made things difficult, it was more just that their shows were such big deals and sometimes it's just a big machine. They had a bunch of assistants and so many managers. It's a big production."

Frank: "Did you know one time I pulled Steven Tyler from under the stage? He was down there crying about some personal thing. He was having a kid or something, and he was crying his face off when the show was supposed to be starting. I pulled him right out of there."

John: "I did not, but that's the kind of thing that just keeps them out of my top three. Let's see, back in the day, Black Oak Arkansas. They were hot in the '70s and they were really nice guys. I was with Lynyrd Skynyrd before the crash. They were a fun group of guys.

"I'd say Kool and the Gang (is) number three. They were fun. They were touring with KC and the Sunshine (Band). They were taking turns being headline acts. One night we would close, and the other night they would close. They were just good guys."

— **Rockstars and Executions** —

Frank and John hang up.

Stab in the dark time. Did you ever do cocaine with Fleetwood Mac?

Frank: "With Stevie, yeah. That was a no-brainer. If you were around her, you were doing cocaine or you weren't around her for too long. They were a peculiar group. There were little glitches in every member of that band.

"Why, you want a weird drug story? Okay, it was me, Bill Snouffer, who was Billy Joel's bodyguard, and Billy Joel. We met The Judge at the concert. This was a Billy Joel concert in Texas. The Judge had come backstage. He was some big shot down there."

Stupid question, but was this person an actual judge, like as in at his 9-to-5 he wore black robes?

"Yes, that is what I am telling you. So the Judge had a couple women with him, and he told Billy Joel about a big party he was having that night and how he would love to have Billy come over. We went.

"Early in the party, before it got real weird, there were a bunch of beautiful women and a couple open bars at this guy's house. But there was this guy there who seemed to be a good friend of The Judge, and he kept trying to put a cowboy hat on Billy Joel. Well, Billy Joel is protective of his hair. Billy Joel does not like anyone fucking with his hair. So this guy puts the hat on Billy once, and Bill Snouffer, who is a big fucking guy, stands up and says, 'That's enough with the fucking hat.' The guy did it again. Bill Snouffer looked at me, then at The Judge, so I picked the guy up at the shoulders, got my face real close to his, and I told him what I'd do if he put that fucking cowboy hat on Billy Joel again. If we were not at a judge's house, I would not have been talking. Billy didn't mind hanging with me and Bill Snoffer 'cause of things like that. We looked out for him, you know?

"We were partying, everyone was partying like crazy. It was a pretty good time for a while. The guy who had been fucking around with the cowboy hat was somebody big-time too. He walked us around like he owned the house. Billy Joel went too because I don't think he wanted to be with that fucking Judge for a second longer. So we go into one room, and it's a guy in his undies hanging from the ceiling. I'm not joking. He was doing some kind of workout thing. We went in another room, and there was a bunch of women having sex, a bunch of women. So the party was kind of a scene, you know? It was crazy. So we were standing with The Judge near this big fireplace, and Billy Joel is looking around the mantel. He's looking for the cocaine. Now, there was so much shit going on in this house, I didn't think much of it when Billy Joel asked The Judge where the fucking cocaine was. Now, The Judge did not take that kindly. He started shouting and hollering about religions and whatever else, so Bill Snouffer, Billy, and I started to scoot out of there real quick. The Judge was joking, it was all a joke. He showed Billy Joel, and they did some cocaine. But we left not long after that. The Judge kept touching Billy Joel, just like at his elbow or whatnot, but Bill Snouffer and I were on high alert—no pun intended—and Billy, it was plain to see, didn't want to be at this party that bad. We scooted for real."

The Judge?

"I saw him on the news once. He's a famous judge."

You showed me the John Jumano trailer. How and why did that happen?

"The guy who was supposed to have lines couldn't handle a gun. I said, 'I know how to handle a gun. I'll shoot the woman, I'll shoot the girl,

— **Rockstars and Executions** —

I'll shoot the dog, but hey, we should do this at night.' If we were doing it for real, there's no way we would do this during the day, I told the guy. The director acted a little scared then, but he said, 'Okay, you're the guy holding the gun then, you're shooting them, and you got the speaking lines.'

"That stuff happened a couple times. They have a lot of movies shot down there. I used to ride around Miami with no shirt on because you know Miami, you know Lincoln Road in South Beach, that's where you cruise. I would be riding a motorcycle or driving one of my cars with no shirt on. A little while ago this was all Cuban town, and then they started shifting people and making condos. A longtime associate of mine is this guy, let's call Robert. He had a car place there on US-1. Back in the day, just around the corner from his shop, there was a camp under the bridge. You know those camps of Cubans? They were bad deals, like concentration camps for Cubans.

"The Mariel Boatlift happened in 1980. See, Robert had moved to the USA from Cuba in 1964 when he was eight years old. His family had the car shop when the boat lift happened. Robert had some family and friends who were in the boat lift, and he hired a lot of those guys. The boat guys are hard-working, and a lot of them are criminals. Later in life, after I was out of things, if we wanted to have some play coke, I would go see Robert. So one night I'm there, and I'm over the whole gangster thing, we're just playing around, doing some toots, having fun. Robert gets a call from a big customer of his; he's gotta go out to Fisher Island. You have to take a ferry there. It's full of the richest of the rich. I think Oprah was the neighbor of the guy we went to see. The guy who had called had a Rolls-Royce. It's a real Rolls, but some of his guys had put a different motor in it, which isn't really smart to do. So this hot shot in his waterfront house was kinda pissed at Robert over the deal, and he wanted to fix things up real quick, so we went there at night. Robert had to take a look at the car, and the owner was real nice. He brings us up to his room after, and he asks if we want to eat. He had his personal chef cook us up something. This guy had yoga stuff all over the walls, and I told him I know a little about it, and this guy is mis-labeling everything he's got on his walls. I told him a little about India and yoga, and he thought I was interesting. He was married to this older woman; well, he was older, but she was an older European actress who had been famous. She was from Monaco. That's the woman that I kill in that little John Jumano film. You know she hit me like seven times in the head with the vase? She couldn't get her lines right. So she kept hitting me with the vase, trying to get her line right. Popped collar and slacks, her husband was the whole picture of Miami rich. He was the producer of this film. He wanted to make it for his wife.

"So I was at the guy's house with Robert, and as we're leaving, he comes over to me and he says, 'Do you want to be in a movie?' I'm looking at him—and this is not the first time—but I'm not interested in making no porno. But no, he sent Robert a script a couple days later. I was supposed to be the muscle part, but I could hold the gun. So when we showed up on set, well, it was his house. We flipped parts. I did another movie for that same guy. It was one where they pretended to throw someone out a helicopter, and I was on the ground and I'm like, 'Oh no, they're throwing my people out that helicopter.'

"When I really stopped being a gangster, I was in Greensboro, North Carolina. I had a yoga place there; it was called The Purple Lotus. It was on Valentine Street. The Woolworth's where the Greensboro sit-in happened was not more than a hundred feet down the road. You know there was a time when the neighborhood kids would get together to listen to a radio show? Only The Shadow knows. As for TV, there was *The Ed Sullivan Show*. Ed would promote James Brown, which was a rarity. He maybe even had the Beatles on and The Stones. We got a lot of what was new from that show."

Frank shows me the screen of his phone, ringing with a call from Dan the Man.

Frank: "Hey man, I'm here with this guy who is writing about what all happened."

Dan the Man: "Ain't nobody going to believe that!"

Frank: "Hey, tell it for my guy here. How did I meet you?"

Dan: "Well, let's see. It was at a gym in Greensboro over on Battleground Avenue. You were working some guys out, and I noticed every time the door opened you had to turn around and look. I'd seen you around. You were driving some stupid bike."

Frank: (laughs) "Fuck you, that thing was pretty."

Dan: "He had put (on) all this chrome shit. I think there were chrome pinwheels at one point. What an asshole. (laughs) Not long after that, I saw him in a Jaguar, and I thought you're in the business. Frankie was the best personal trainer I'll ever have. I work out with anyone else, and I'm firing them in five minutes."

Frank: "We got to being buddies during those sessions."

Dan: "Yup. See, I was in the oil and gas industry, and I had spent a lot of time in Colombia. I had set some friends from home up with some guys, and they were doing some stuff. So Frank went in, and we did some work together."

Frank: "That was just about it for me. We had some fun though."

Dan: "I got a guy down there now negotiating with the government of Colombia. It's a fucking mess, they're not producing shit. The government wants some independents to come down and fix it. So Frankie, I was calling to say, you got anything planned? You got any interest in coming to Cartagena with me next month?"

Frank: "I'm going to have to give that some thought. That's exciting."

Dan: "The adventure is never over, brother. It just starts again."

Frank: "Alright, brother, take care. I'll talk to you really soon."

Dan: "You got it. And hey, writer man, be sure to tell everyone this guy drove the ugliest fucking motorcycle you have ever seen. That shoulda been a crime."

They're laughing riotously as they disconnect. Frank's face sinks a bit when the call ends. For just a second there I had that feeling I've not had since high school, where you walk into a room and you've got a big dumb grin plastered on your face; you're ready to have fun, only by accident you've walked into the wrong party and the wrong scene. The drugs are not what you expected, the crowd is older, there's something more serious going on here, and you realize that you, you are here by accident. I felt that twinge of fear and excitement again, of being on the edge of deep shit and liking it, for just a minute there. Then I saw Frank's expression when they disconnected.

Frank: "You asked if I like Brian Wilson? Yes. Brian was a nice enough guy. I was with them on the whole Flip-Flop Tour, which is pretty late in their careers, although they're probably still touring and that was maybe, what, forty fucking years ago? So I don't know that 'late career' is the right term. But you see, by that point, they had been very famous and very rich for a long time. Brian was a strange guy, you know? Heavy alcohol and drug user. His brother, the drummer, loved the pills and the cocaine. Brian would do some cocaine, but he loved downers and he loved to drink. They tipped me out eighteen-hundred dollars, I think, at the end of the tour. I liked that whole group. I did their security at a couple shows at places like (the College of) William & Mary in the years after, kind of a special gig because we all got along so well on the tour. But they had a distant eye, do you know what I mean? [No] They wanted to entertain, but they lost the fire, they lost the kick. They lost the fire, you know what I mean? They got distant. We called it being french fried, where, you know, he lost that energy kick—it's the drugs. Being french fried? Paul McCartney supposedly didn't like singing the old songs, but he would put on a show. He never did this. Brian Wilson wasn't like that. He did lose the heat. Do you know how important it is to not have the distant eye? Your eyes need to feel and be felt."

Well, since we're going a bit deeper. When I was a practicing alcoholic, I had a way of looking down on anyone who wouldn't drink around me. Did you have a chip on your shoulder around people who weren't buying from you?

Frank: "I liked sober people. Correction, I loved being around sober people. Because I could count on them. I did not like doing business with the people around me, I just did it. When I could, I worked with family. When I couldn't, I worked with people I had a long-time rapport with. When I couldn't, I pretty much stopped working, you know? Look, marijuana is whatever, but it doesn't really change you, I don't think. Cocaine changes you. I sold a lot, and I mean *a lot*, of marijuana, and I am fine with that. People on cocaine cannot be trusted. I don't care who they are. I didn't barely trust myself. That's how things go from goofy to real fucking bad.

"I smoked cocaine twice. You know that makes it harder, stronger, worse? I'll say it again, do not do fucking business with people on cocaine."

When you were on tour, were you and the other bodyguards responsible for procuring girls?

Frank: "Well, the bands pretty much all had their own guy. It's not a bodyguard. Usually, it's a person who started with a band and stays with them. You don't even need to be a bodyguard or a music label guy. If you're with the band when they're growing up and you're willing to help them get what they want, those type of people get to stick around. It's the ones who say no, never, that are just cut right out. So there's a lot to it, the way women would get backstage. I met the Eagles once, and it was pretty much just like you're saying. But most bands and most big shows, there's a lot going on, and a lot of what's going on is beautiful women who want to feel like a rock star too. Yeah, some of those guys who hung around bands were there to make sure there were girls."

I did not hear the phone start ringing this time.

Frank: "Hey Ricky, when did you meet me?"

Ricky the Hat: "We got into a little bit of a fight. Um, this was at the shipyard. But if you mean like as friends, you met me at the Harley-Davidson shop sometime after the dustup, and we took a ride. We were just kids really."

Frank: "Oh shit, that's right. We hung out at the bike shop. Then we started doing some business together after?"

Rick: "That is correct."

Frank: "Hey, so I'm with a writer guy. He's putting all this shit down. Can you tell him about The Renegades?"

Rick: "Alright, sure. Well, we had some things in common. We all liked bikes and cars. We all liked rock and roll, and money too."

Frank: "Now, before I started selling marijuana with you, I said I was gonna make an amount of money and then get the fuck out. Do you remember that?"

Rick: (laughs) "Yes, I do. You said you were gonna make ten thousand bucks, and then you were going to quit the business. You did say that. We're just doing this long enough to get a little money, all of us."

Frank: "There was (redacted), and (redacted). But do you remember the guy we called Buffoon?"

Rick: (laughs) "Sure."

Frank: "The Buffoon and I got tight. We started splashing cash and taking the stupidity to a new level. He was the one who came to me and said, 'I got a deal: you and Ricky the Hat are gonna go to the place in New York.' We were gonna go rob these people and make a whole bunch of money, that was the plan. I remember I said, 'Ricky, we are in the marijuana business. We are in the pill business. We're not in the robbery business.' I got pretty pissed."

Rick: "Yeah, you said that wasn't us. You had it right."

Frank: "So tell him what happened."

Rick: "Well, so some Renegades and our buddy Paul take on the job. Next thing you know, Paul was in the news and they were all hiding up in the Catskills or whatever. See, they tied up the people—a guy and his wife—and they strangled the guy to get him to tell them where the stuff was. They killed him. And some neighbor or whatever caught on to what was happening, they got into a chase, and Paul got nabbed. I remember one of the guys I knew from the Renegades. I saw him much later on and he had gotten frostbite hiding up in some mountains. He had lost a bunch of toes."

Frank: "Let me give you one more name. See if you remember this: Willie the Cue."

Rick: "Willie Truelove. Oh yeah!"

Frank: "Now, what do you think about that?"

Rick: (laughs) "He is about as crazy as they come."

Frank: "When Willie got out of the penitentiary he came to my house in Miami, and he put a line of cocaine about three fingers wide down the entire length of my dining table. He had been out of prison for about half a morning, and he put a marker halfway down the dining room table and points to his side of the table and says, 'This is my half.' I said, 'First of all, you goofy son of a bitch, this is my house!'"

Rick: (laughs) "I bet he did his half too."

Frank: "Hey, last one: Did you and me ever go to Miami together?"

Rick: "Yeah, we went to Miami once."

Frank: "What did we do there?"

Rick: "Well, we were on the edge of something big, you can say that."

Frank: "Who did we go see?"

Rick: "Nah, man. I'll talk to you later."

The phone call ends.

Frank: "Who cares? It was Pablo Escobar. He was in Miami, but he wasn't supposed to be in the country at all. My friend Gilbert introduced us. We met in a club. It was real casual. Escobar was meeting Gilbert and some of the Cubans, and Ricky and I were there. They talked for ten, maybe fifteen minutes, and then one of Escobar's guys says he has to go because officially he was not there, you know? That was it. It wasn't a big deal.

"I had a friend who I played football with in high school. He went into the service and was stationed in Germany, and he married a German girl. When he came home, he needed money, and he was reliable. I helped him buy a house in Bowers Hill, near where my parents lived, and his house was one of my warehouses, if you want to call it that. He had a good-sized garage, and a kilo of cocaine is not that big of a thing. When we were dealing more in marijuana, then space was more of an issue.

"Here's the golden rule when it comes to dealing drugs: you don't take fifty kilos to your town if it's only a five-kilo town. Do you understand? The ship yard, Norfolk and Virginia Beach, that's a really big area and a lot of people. Five kilos there and it's not that much—it's not enough really—but then in another place at the same time five kilos is a shitload. It's all about where you're at, how many people are buying whole kilos from you, and how fast you can move the rest. You don't want to hold onto the bomb for too long; a smart business man minimizes the time he spends holding a bomb.

"Let's say we wanted to start a little drug network here in Surf City today. We'll start small. You go in there to the bars and look around, have a drink, whatever, and eventually let it be known that if anyone is looking for weed, coke, pills, I'm your guy, and you slide over a gram of the best coke in the world. That's why bars are easy. You can slide them the gram, nobody gets a whiff of it and I do mean whiff of it. Because the real coke, the stuff before we cut it, you can feel it on your fingers; shit, you'll feel it all the way to your toes. There is nothing in the world like high-grade cocaine. I don't care if you already got a guy who can get you shit, he cannot get you this stuff. So you go to a couple bars, and you say. 'If you need to get with me, here's where you reach me.' You keep your guys out of the picture. They're just off doing their thing. Then you call them in, and they're there to watch my fucking door. They're watching for people watching me, and if they need to, they're grabbing anyone. No fucking around, just in and out. If it's heat, you get out of there, but if it's not, guess what? That town is yours now. And remember what I said about a five-kilo town? Well, this might be a five-kilo town. Do you know how much money you can turn over when you're taking your five kilos, cutting it to ten, and then working it? That's a lot of money. But that's small, and that's a great way to get pinched. What you do is make friends and just sell the five keys in one deal. That's how you make the real money: you don't need to know anyone, you're not doing any of the work moving it around, it's done. That's when you make the real money.

"So if I gave you an ounce, I would say cut it with another ounce—vitamin A, whatever—because this shit is high-test. You take a knife, and you stick it into the kilo package, and you try to feel the oil on your fingers. Then you taste it, just a pinhead. Because this shit is high-test, the oils will push together. You can feel the buzz through your fingers, brother."

Day Seven

Kathleen

Kathleen walks in playing a song on her phone. I look at the decorations in the room while she plays "U Said" by Jimmy Dennis. Who decorated this room?

"It was my idea, but I wasn't moving too good at the time. I was insistent about the Kennedy photos."

In addition to magazine covers from Kitty's legal career and letters of commendation that accompanied academic awards, there are a group of photos of the Kennedy family—Jackie and the kids, American Camelot.

"Troy Anthony Davis was a tragic case. Troy was innocent, but unfortunately he was black, and the prosecutors would not give up on him being guilty. Another African-American male, (Sylvester) 'Redd' Coles, confessed to the crime, but his confession was treated as hearsay. Unlike Jimmy Dennis, where after a while the prosecutors listened to us, they just refused to look at Troy Anthony's appeals. My appeals all failed. I felt horrible, like the world is still not aware of the innocents that are in prison. That just made me feel terrible for a while. I myself got Pope Benedict the XVI to appeal for a new trial for Troy.

— Rockstars and Executions —

"Race was an issue in death row innocence cases, and poverty too; Roger was a coal miner from West Virginia. There is a wealth issue in our justice system. I don't think I'm the first to point that truth out. The other bane of the justice system is the system of jailhouse confessions. They are almost entirely false. Even if the confessor is being honest, the confessee has been shown time and again to exaggerate what the confessor is confessing to. Jailhouse confessions are almost always some form of lie, and the motives for the lies are right there for all to see."

Of your three innocence cases, were they good people in your estimation?

Kathleen: "Roger was an asshole and a jerk. He was cocky. He had lots of girlfriends even though he was married. He was Mister Self-Proclaimed Popularity. Jimmy Dennis was nice. He was part of the 'in' clique at prison, so he was a tough guy. So did I know if someone like Jimmy was a criminal of a different sort? I know it sounds arrogant, but I could tell immediately. Jimmy, for example, might have been a bad man, a gangster, but the crime that landed him on death row? He was innocent of it, and I knew it.

"I worked just as hard for all of them, regardless of their personality, but if they acted tough I would try to break them down. I would try to get them to see that they are no better than anyone else. They seemed to enjoy me joking with them because to them it seemed to be the final indicator that I took them seriously. Sometimes it felt like I wasn't trusted until we were able to communicate on that level. I would flirt with the men on death row as a means to work them, unsettle them, to probe their innocence or relative bullshittiness.

"I did in one instance talk to a guy who claimed his innocence, and I knew right away. I didn't leave until I had his confession to the crime. That, to me, was part of my due diligence. How terrible would it be to represent a guilty person and get them off?

"Even if I didn't think someone like Roger was the greatest person, I would prefer him on the street than in jail. Yeah, I do. If you want to know what Roger Coleman's life was like, look up a book called *May God Have Mercy* by John Tucker. It's not so straightforward a story. But with Roger, in my gut I felt he was not completely trustworthy. I felt if he was on the street he was going to be a piece of shit pretty soon. Jimmy Dennis just wanted to sing and be with his family. Jimmy and Troy were different."

*****

Interlude

Normally, Kathleen will exit The Confessional as Frank enters, ships passing in the night. Today, Frank touches her arm, asks her if she's ready, and says, "We gotta do it sometime." Frank and Kathleen enter The Confessional. Frank asks the questions, I start typing, unsure what's happening.

Frank: "How many houses did you have when you were way out there on the alcohol?"

Kathleen: "My place in Founders Park, in Old Town Alexandria. Then I had a house on Tilghman Island, a kinda rundown farmhouse. I loved it. I kayaked all around there. Then I had a house in Easton, Maryland. I got that house because I was dating a nice rich guy and I wanted to be close to him."

Frank: "Did you know your houses were being trashed?"

— Rockstars and Executions —

Kathleen: "Yeah, the house on Tillman Island was first. A friend of a friend took it over, and by the time I saw it, it was no longer livable. I lost the place in Alexandria after the medical bills from the first couple strokes wiped me out. Then the Easton house got trashed. I stayed up in my room drinking, and drug dealers were downstairs. I no longer knew who these people were, they were dangerous guys, and they'd just be there in my living room. I'd walk right past them, and I would walk straight as I could down the street to the liquor store. It was about twenty houses away. I'd buy vodka, and I'd come home to drink it down."

Frank: "Did you ever call the law on the drug dealers in your house?"

Kathleen: "I did eventually. It just got too crazy, it forced me to wake up. I walked to the police station, and I told them that I am an alcoholic who is going into treatment and about the squatters at my house. While I was in treatment, Easton police would drive by my house five times a night to prevent them from showing back up."

Frank: "How long were you in the hospital for, before they let you out to go to a treatment center?"

Kathleen: "I was in the hospital for four weeks. I fell into a coma."

Frank: "You said you saw something when you woke up?"

Kathleen: "All I saw was everything was white. I felt like I was in this completely white room. Honestly, I thought I had gone to heaven. it was creepy as hell."

Frank: "Alright Kitty, good shit. Get outta here now. It's time for the star to shine, you know?" (laughs)

Kathleen: (laughs) "I'm going to walk to the beach later today."

Frank: "She will. You watch, she fucking will."

— Andrew Mallin —

*****

Frank

"That's why I picked this room for us to meet in every time, it felt right. I wasn't here when she decorated it in here, but I knew right away, this space was hers. She lost her last couple houses. She doesn't own this one. Her life was a mess. She got so fucked up, and there were people partying like crazy, destroying her homes, and she didn't know she was at the party. Kitty was friends with a cousin of mine a while back—my cousin, she's another lawyer—and when things went really bad for Kitty, she helped her get her affairs in order. I was working at a treatment center, I did yoga there, and I had done personal recovery work before. It became pretty clear to me that Kitty was going to be my big project, you know? This big thing I was going to do right. So, sorry about all that, but she's been waiting to say it for a while, and she needed to say it. We'll walk to the beach later, and she'll talk about it. I'm not taking that little fucking dog with us though.

"So you wanted to talk about how long I was in jail for? Okay, well, I came back from India with two passports and two drivers licenses. I didn't go home, I landed in New York, and I got a hotel room at the Waldorf Astoria. I waited seven days, just ordering room service, doing a thousand push-ups a day. I waited that long because if I was going to get popped I wanted it to go down there and not with family or business.

"I tell you, when I got off that plane from India I was moving like a rocket ship I was so nervous. There was a beautiful woman on the plane, and so as we were exiting the plane, I just kept my eyes on her and acted like I was talking to her real normal, like we were a couple excited about making plans, and I don't remember what I said, but I was just kinda saying things to appear normal, and I fucking sprinted out of that terminal once we were off the plane.

"After seven days, I called a cousin, and he is supposed to pick me up, only I forgot to tell him my alias name. I was 'Anthony Bruno,' so he couldn't find me. The concierge knocked on my door. I was freaking the fuck out. I would've jumped out the window, only it's the concierge with my cousin. He had described me by appearance, you know?

"I couldn't go to my house. I had my cousin drive me to my girlfriend's place. This is in Virginia too. I had twins with this woman. It took her forever to answer the door because she was selling a little bit out of the house. When I was knocking, she was in the bathroom flushing. She nearly fell over when she saw it was me, and then without a word she was up to her shoulder in the toilet.

"I had lost almost everything, but there were people who owed me money and I had some hidden money. We had hidden coke too. Four kilos. So I took the cash and said to my girlfriend, let's go buy a used car in her name. We got a Cadillac because it's got a big trunk. So I sent my girlfriend to get the car titled, and I'm there at her place with the twins. They're toddlers, they're crying, time was going pretty slow. I was racing back and forth between the back and front doors. I was nervous as shit. The phone rang, and Donna had been shot.

"Now, my mind went to a place. There were a bunch of people who owed me money and had for a couple years. I thought this was my doing. Nope. She had shot herself in the foot. So the story was my girlfriend carried a four-shot .357 derringer in her purse. When she walked into the DMV, her purse got snagged on the door, the derringer hit the ground and went off. In a fucking DMV, she had shot herself in the foot—the quiet buildings where you go to get your license. Well, as you can imagine, it was quite the scene. She was sent to (the) hospital finally. I went and saw Donna and made sure she was okay. I talked to Donna, and I was explaining to her what to do with the attorney should any problem with the gun comes up when this doctor told me I shouldn't be in there. I wanted to fucking throttle him, but I left.

"About a year ago, an associate of mine had buried four kilos by a tree on the edge of the swamp. It took me and my cousin over three hours to find that shit. And it was mostly ruined coke. But it was smart to hide it. When we found it, my cousin did a dance, kilos over his head. I needed that shit, needed to build up a cash fund. But I got popped the next day. I went to see my wife. I had no place to go really.

"I had an uncle who had been a local cop, so when they brought me into the Chesapeake police station, I saw some cops; some had worked with me, and some of them fucking hated me. My lawyer was allowed to see me. I asked him for some pills: downers, you know? So he sent a doctor to come see me in the jail, and the doctor gave me a bunch of Valium."

Why'd you want the Valium?

Frank: "I was freaking out. I was revved up. I was too worked up. I was worried about the charges I was facing. I was worried about girlfriends and my wife. I had my bond set at eight hundred grand. I wanted to pay bond and just get the fuck out of the country again. I didn't have to. I paid the prosecutor two hundred fifty grand in a briefcase and gave him the title to two Jaguars, and I spent seven days in jail. I was a wanted felon with a history of trafficking cocaine, but all the evidence was shaky. I don't know; this guy just wanted some money and cars. The particulars of which were two hundred and fifty thousand dollars and two Jaguars. I couldn't fucking believe it. It wiped me out. I mean every little coffee can—empty, done—but I spent seven days in jail. I've spent eight days in jail in my entire life.

"The first time I should have gone to jail was when the Quaalude King ratted me out. I did not like the Quaaludes because it fucks people up so much; lot of people getting in car wrecks and stupid shit like that because they're so out of it on them fucking things. It's not a good drug. That's a bad drug because actually in Miami kids were dying because they look like these Smarties candies. Anyway, I took a million of them from him and I sold them. I remember there was this one minor league baseball team. I went to their practice field one day, and I saw all their cars in the parking lot, but I couldn't see any of the players. Normally, you can hear them playing. Look, they were laying down on the baseball field, everyone of 'em zonked out on fucking Quaaludes. So I said shit on this, I wanted out of there. You can buy them for twenty-five cents apiece, and you can sell them for five bucks a piece. So they're small, they're not heavy or bulky, and off a couple thousand pills you can make a shitload of money. It's a great way to make money, but I hate that drug.

"So I saw the Quaalude King in the courtroom. You want to hear something funny? He didn't remember that he had just fucking ratted me out. He greeted me just as warm as can be, like we're fucking buddies who are happy to see each other, and I'm like, 'Hey man, are you kidding me? You are the one who fucking told these people my name. You are why we are in bracelets. Are you kidding me?' His lawyer hustled him away after that. He was wearing one of them Scottish rigs—I remember that—he looked like an idiot, but it was his way of dressing up.

"The second time I got pinched though, I had to walk up to the judge

— Andrew Mallin —

and just say 'I'm guilty.' Well, instinct kicked in. I walked forward, the judge asks me if I'm guilty, and I said, 'No sir, I am not guilty.' Well, my lawyer shit an absolute brick, the prosecutor was hollering. I remember my lawyer and I huddled next to these big flags, and my lawyer wanted to know what the fuck was I doing? He's like, 'All you have to fucking say is I'm guilty and this fucking judge is going to give you probation and a suspended fucking sentence, do not fuck this up.' I said, 'Sorry, I'm just used to saying not guilty whenever anyone asks about anything.' I might've been a little goofy on them Valium. So the judge brings me back in front once things are going again. And he says, 'Let's try this again, are you guilty?' I said, 'I plead guilty,' and my lawyers let out their breath they'd been holding."

Day Eight

Kathleen

Why did you want to work the death row innocence cases?

"I wanted to work death penalty cases in general since I was a law student doing work for the NAACP. So I worked several cases there and got one guy off death row who was a non-shooter. I wanted to work death penalty cases full-time, but there were no hiring's for that role. I went to Arnold & Porter because they occasionally took on pro bono death penalty cases; it was the best I could've hoped for."

How did you end up working for the NAACP?

"I had a Columbia professor (named) James Liebman, who was a famous NAACP practitioner. He actually paid me some money to work on this thing called the *Habeas Corpus Manual*. That's when he asked me if I'd like to work on a death case, and I said sure. Jack Boger is a lawyer down here, but at the time he was in New York, and he started the death penalty project at the NAACP. He was one of the kindest people I ever met."

Were you involved in innocence cases where the defendant wasn't on death row?

"Yes. You're asking about 'police conduct' cases because they do things like say a person has confessed, will brook people into saying things they didn't say, will back them into corners without a lawyer present, will take care of mental deficiencies. There was a guy in Baltimore; he had committed no crime, and they talked him into being convicted of multiple additional charges. He was just some guy who had gotten beaten up, and they put a couple assaults and armed robberies on him. He thought even without the conviction being proven he had lost too much—he'd already been fired, his name was in the papers—and he killed himself in Baltimore Prison. There was another guy in Alabama who had mental health issues, and the cops there leaned on those issues to make him admit to things he didn't do. He was batshit crazy. This was a person who couldn't hold a conversation, and they accused him of committing organized and calculated crimes. It would've been one thing if they had put him in a sanatorium, but they put him in a maximum security jail where he couldn't get any mental health professional help, despite our best efforts, and he died in jail."

What's his name?

"I can't tell you; he has family living."

*****

Frank

As Kathleen walks out, she calls to Frank that it's his turn. "How was it?" he wants to know. "You're good?" he asks her. "I'm good," she says. After she leaves, I remark that Kathleen strikes me as someone who no longer has an interest in alcohol.

"Correct, she does not want that shit anymore. No more. Now it's the pills. She doesn't want any pills—give her credit, she genuinely does not want them—but her fucking caregivers care for her with pills. She has frontal lobe problems, okay? I only met her two, three years ago. So I have this female cousin I have a complicated history with. She knows what I've been up to, but she trusts me because she knows in the last couple years I had a couple good experiences helping people get clean. Plus, I've been training and training people my whole life."

Do you think you should be in jail?

"Yeah. Yeah. But I corrected myself, somewhat. (laughs) When you're a gangster, it's like you have these five personalities, the five faces. I'll tell you one. I'm standing with a big-time gangster at my house on Chic's Beach one day. This was in the summer sometime, and we were throwing some fireworks—cherry bombs and stuff like that—and this guy looks at me all serious. He was very concerned. He goes, 'Don't you know fireworks are illegal?' He was worried about the police over some fireworks. Now, this is a guy who I had picked up about a week previous from a warehouse. He'd called me all agitated as shit, and when he got in the car he said he was in a killing mood. He was fucking fired up. I asked him what happened. He had his pistol out, and he was cranking lines of coke. He was crazy, pointing his gun everywhere out the car window, and he's almost pointing it at me, and he says, 'I don't care who,' he just needs to do some killing. So I'm yelling, 'What the fuck is up?' Well, his dog had died."

Dog fighting?

"No, his fucking dog just died, it was an old boy. (laughs) I talked him out of doing anything too crazy that night.

"Should I be in jail? Maybe not for the marijuana, but for the cocaine? Yes, I should be in jail for it. But I should say I didn't know what cocaine was really before I started moving it. Then again, I fucked with a couple ounces of it in Norfolk after the ELO show. This was before I met Gilbert Hernandez and all them GQ-looking motherfuckers in Miami. Gilbert's guy worked at Miami airport for DHL. That was one of the best connections in the civilized world. Kilos were coming in, and we were just walking out the back door. That gas station next to the back gate of Miami airport had more fucking coke in it than Studio 54."

When was the first time you bought a kilo?

"It was two kilos. Bill Snouffer called from where he was on the tour with Black Sabbath. I was a marijuana dealer and I was in the marijuana business. Bill Snouffer worked real close with this big promoter, Steve Gudis, and Gudis was telling Bill this stuff is the future. I was the hashish, marijuana, and Quaaludes guy. So Bill says, 'If you want to sell this shit, I'll hook you up with my friend in Miami.' Bill was talking about how much money we can make with this coke shit, how he has this primo connection in Miami. This is the rise of Gilbert Hernandez and Pete Gonzalez. A gangster has several girlfriends, he gets out of the area where he's working, so going to the movies in the next town over was always alright. And the night Bill Snouffer called to say we could meet the guy who ended up being Gilbert, I was at the movies with my girlfriend, and we were watching this movie called *The Blue Brothers*, and there was this line in the movie—it went something like, "We're on a mission from God"—and I was thinking about that business offer of Bill's. At first, I was hesitant. I was in the marijuana business, but I thought about that line and it seemed like, I dunno, maybe the time is now. So I talked to Bill the next day, and

— Andrew Mallin —

I met Gilbert Hernandez not long after that.

"Gilbert Hernandez was partners with Pete Gonzalez and Bobby Gonzalez. I honestly forget if any of them were actually brothers, but they all said they were brothers. Pete and Bobby were real tight and they were more like muscle. All three of them worked for Uncle Nikolai. We can talk about him because he's dead.

"Uncle Nikolai was Colombian, so this was not exactly that kind of family. Uncle is the one who gave me the name Mister Loco. It's Bobby Gilbert, me, and the Uncle in one of my cars, and Uncle doesn't speak a lot of English, and I'm driving, and the guys (are) in the backseat. We're on I-95, and Uncle points, 'We're going the wrong way.' So I said, 'I'll flip it around. You want me to flip around? I'm a good driver, I'll flip it around.' Now, none of them knew what I meant. [Neither do I.] So they don't really understand what I'm saying, but Bobby in the back seat is like, 'Fuck yea, man, flip it around!' So I went down in the gully between the interstates and whipped the car around."

You pulled a U-turn on the highway?

"Yea, with a big bump in between the two directions. So I made the turn at speed. and the guys they were laughing, and Uncle is saying quietly, 'Loco, loco.' So that's how I got that nickname."

Did you feel friendly with any of the bands?

"A lot of them were friendly."

Is that because they knew you had drugs?

"Yeah, probably. It would be a tie probably between The Beach Boys and The Doobie Brothers. Lot of nice guys in both setups. The Rolling Stones were very friendly with me because I knew my boundaries with them—I didn't really talk at all around them, and I wasn't pestering them for an autograph or anything. Alice Cooper was a real friendly guy. He was not what I expected. A lot of the country bands were friendly. But The Doobie Brothers were probably the nicest. they got along with their road crew and everything. That's not common."

Did any of the acts train with you?

"The only one that liked to train was David Lee Roth from Van Halen. Him and Bill Snouffer were kickers; they were big into doing these high-kick martial arts. They would see me stretching or working out, and sometimes they got into it too. Mick Jagger was into stretching; he might not want to break a sweat, but he liked the stretching. Bruce Springsteen worked out with me one day. I forget what we did, but I remember he was a guy in jeans in the gym. Other than that, Bruce was like a normal guy. The bodyguard for New Kids on the Block trained with me. He was a friend, and he was busy as shit because he was also the bodyguard for Blackstreet and Blackstreet were just as hot as New Kids. Those were two acts that got real hot around the same time. That bodyguard was a good hitter; I forget his name. Here's how the math works around a band: let's say there are five guys in the band, then there's twenty guys to take care of them, you've got ten family members hanging around, and then there's the crowd and the serious fans. Some of the band members, some acts, they are introverts, even with all this going on, does that make sense? The point is there is a lot going on, and when the band members are introverted like that they're even more crazy on stage."

Frank shows me the phone screen after hitting send. He is calling "Big Hitter Blackstreet." No answer.

"This guy was a gopher in the business when he got started—he would go get things for the bands. Then he contacted me when I was in

— **Andrew Mallin** —

Greensboro, and he had made it. He was managing Jodeci. He's a solid guy, he's from Virginia Beach. You might not know it, but there's a whole bunch of acts that are from that area: Missy Elliott, 2 Live Crew were from right down the road [...Miami], and a whole bunch of other performers were from Virginia Beach. There's a recording studio in Virginia Beach that all kinds of music acts went there for. I know these people. So four years ago, Shawn, this guy who watches all these acts, says, 'There's this big show, and I need people.' That's the last show I worked. Four years ago. I was pretty much seventy years old and working the front stage, watching the climbers from the pit, and keeping the front of the stage clear. It was a two-day gig. 2 Live Crew came out, and they had that place going nuts. I kind of miss that."

Day Nine

Kathleen

Kathleen is otherwise occupied when I arrive and sleeping in the sun on her deck when I leave.

*****

Frank

Frank plays the Chelo "Cha Cha" music video on YouTube.

"Chelo was a friend of mine. His label got bought by Gloria Estefan and her husband, Emilio. Chelo was a bit of a heavy drug user, but he was a star in the making. Then he got blacklisted from the recording studio for his drug use. They had sold him the drugs. It happened in every field, in ever profession. It's probably still happening. That's what I call a double standard."

Did any of the acts strike you as tough?

"David Lee Roth could handle himself in a fight, for sure. He was pretty well trained in martial arts, and he took it serious. Mostly no, though.

— Rockstars and Executions —

Most of the bands had guys for that sort of thing. Billy Idol had a lot of energy, and he didn't take being messed around. I didn't know if he could fight, but he did not seem afraid to try. And then Billy Joel."

The Piano Man could fight?

"Well, I don't know if he's going to win any prizes, but he was a boxer at one time. None of those guys are killers, if you know what I mean, but Billy Joel could box pretty good.

"I'm trying to think of this guy. He was in country music, archery— Ted Nugent, that's the guy. He was good with hunting and knives and shit. Here's a story for you. So one show I needed extra guys to work the barrier right in front of the stage. That's the least fancy work, you're just kicking the shit out of anyone who tries to go over the barrier. So I see this guy— we called him Oil Guy; he wore some hair product or whatever in his beard, the thing glistened. This guy was huge and buffed, real big guy, and he had this weird necklace on. It was a dog collar like the guys in the service, but this one had spikes on it. So I saw this guy and said, 'Do you want to work rock and roll security with me?' I used to carry this briefcase around during shows; the briefcase is full of drugs. Sometimes I would ask someone working for me to carry the briefcase. So Oil Man is carrying the briefcase for me the night of a Ted Nugent show, and we go see Ted Nugent before the concert, and Ted Nugent had an archery target all set up. I guess he would fire off some bow and arrows before a show to relax. So I forget if it was my idea or Ted's, but we had the Oil Man stand in front of the target with an apple on his head, and this guy is a big dude, he blocks the target entirely. Well, Ted shot off an arrow . . . and the Oil Man never moved a muscle. He didn't even twitch. We're crazy but we're not that crazy. I told Ted to shoot an arrow in another direction. I'm pretty sure the Oil Man never would've moved even if we shot an arrow right at him.

"Real, real early in my career, I gave my friend John a bunch of marijuana to sell. John was Billy Joel's bodyguard. So John had a duffel bag full of weed, and he's at this house where one of Billy Joel's ex-girlfriends is pissed at Billy, and they somehow or another send the cops, and John is in the upstairs bathroom, and he fucking chucks this duffel bag of weed into the trees. Thing got stuck there, so once the cops were gone they tried everything to get it down. I think they had to finally call a cherry picker to get a duffel bag of weed out of a tree, with Billy Joel serenading them pretty much the whole time.

"John toured with KC and The Sunshine band before he was Billy Joel's bodyguard. KC owned a shitload of parrots, and one of them bit John bad. That shit was hilarious."

The phone rings.

Frank: "Hey sweetie pie, I'm here with the story man. Can you tell him when did you first hear my name?"

Tammy: "I was sixteen, and my boyfriend at the time, his dad owned a car place, and my boyfriend's dad was painting a big Pantera with a custom paint job. And he said he was painting this for Frankie Sumner. I was sixteen then and I'm 56 now, so let's call it forty years."

Frank: "And like, how did you know me? What was I like?"

Tammy: "There were a lot of your cars at that place, maybe five or six of Franks cars were there to be customized or painted. My boyfriend's father didn't say anything that I remember, but I understood pretty quickly what line of work Frank was in."

Frank: "Hey sweetie pie, I'll call you later, alright? Bye. [The call disconnects.] She's a beautiful woman. A very beautiful woman."

— Rockstars and Executions —

Would you marry her?

Frank: "Oh, hell no! I've been married enough times. No, we're good. A marriage is like a piano on tour. When you move a fucking piano on tour you have to tune it, every time. It's a lot of fucking work. Piano sounds great, it's the centerpiece, it's what it's all about, you know? But it's a lot of work. There was this guy, Charlie the Tuner. He was a fucking drug nut, but he was there on tours just to tune the pianos."

Were there any acts that seemed to dislike the fans?

Frank: "Aerosmith sometimes. Actually, let's take that back. They were edgy about fans, very edgy. They were definitely against anyone on the barricade watching them. Confusing, right? Well, Aerosmith meant the security guards. They didn't want them looking towards the stage. They would yell at the security guards to look the other fucking way. Steven Tyler spit a lot, he would spit towards the crowd. Mick Jagger was a guy who was edgy like that, and for good reason. There were a lot of bottles thrown back then, and these are supposedly his fans. But they're fucking nuts, some fans.

"I remember Bob Marley, then later Peter Tosh opened for the Rolling Stones, and some of the Stones fans were really not there to listen to a black artist. It was a while ago. Anyway, you'd see some fucking idiots losing their shit about Bob Marley or Peter Tosh. These guys would throw heavy shit like a Jack Daniels bottle. I remember, I think it was Bob Marley playing, but it might've been Peter Tosh, and this guy threw a bottle. We found the guy. There was a big pond behind the coliseum, and we dragged him right out to the pond, and we beat the shit out of him. I remember [he doesn't] Peter Tosh or Bob really appreciated that. They found some of us in black shirts after the show and thanked us for hauling that fucking cracker out of there. You'd be surprised by how angry people get at these shows they're supposed to be having fun at.

"You asked if some acts stunk out the joint? One show that people started walking out on was Sting. And another show that people walked out on was Rod Stewart. With Rod, he was worn out from touring. He was limp. And another show people walked out on was U2, which sounds fucked up, but they just didn't have it that night. That's what some people don't know about touring: it's like going to war. Some days you have the fight in you, and some days you can't pick up your weapon. (With) Sting, people were walking out in packs. Sinead O'Connor was doing good, and then she made a comment about babies or the Pope . . . abortion? People lost their shit and started booing her like crazy. They hated her after that. I thought she was a real good singer, she had a great voice. This was around '87, "Nothing Compares 2 U" was a big hit. I remember that song. I also remember she had a big fucking mouth. I don't think other people there appreciated her thoughts."

U2 bombed a live show?

Frank: "Yeah, there's no good way to explain it because they're one of the biggest bands in the world, and they were right on top of it then. But yeah, this one night at the Arena they put on a crappy show. They sounded like shit, and people started walking out, and Bono was yelling at them. I remember Bono did not like that people were leaving middle of their set, but it's just one show. Everyone has them. Man, those were good times for rock and roll though, and I thought I knew them all, if just in passing because of the drugs. I'd been working for a while, and I made big money in the marijuana business, and I was around the bands, but it wasn't until cocaine came along that I would think, 'Hey, I'm kinda friends with some of

— Rockstars and Executions —

these guys,' because now they wanted me around because of the cocaine.

"I remember Prince had a bad show in Miami, and my buddy and associate Bill Snouffer was his main bodyguard, and Prince had a bad show, and he was pissed. He freaked out, he took off and went to this beach in Brazil, all because a couple of drunken idiots were booing him at one show. So he went and he hid on this beach in Brazil, and Bill asked if I wanted to go with them. I said, 'Fuck no.' I didn't want to hang around that weird little fucker any more than I had to."

Did Prince buy drugs from you?

"No, he was not a druggie then. I know for a fact that he did not take drugs then because Snouffer was his bodyguard. He wouldn't touch coke, he wouldn't take any drugs. Then later in life I heard he got hurt. He did all those dance moves, and all that jumping around isn't easy. I heard he was hurt, and that's what opened the door to pills later in life."

So why didn't you like being around him?

"He was just different. He didn't laugh at any of my jokes. He talked funny. He was a quiet guy. He was probably a pretty smart guy, and we were, well, it was the '80s! It's funny how things happen. The '80s were rolling brother. I don't think I slept for a whole year. I had so much business going on I couldn't stop, the '80s were crazy."

Did you ever have reason to think Griselda "Mama" Blanco or Pablo Escobar might be pissed at you? What was that like?

Frank: "I didn't know him as much. I only met him once and briefly. I've maybe spent a half hour with him in my life. But the Cubans started doing work with him, and the price of kilos stayed down. He was good at what he did.

"Mama I knew from the rooster fights. It felt like a big deal for a gringo to be there. I stood out. The rooster fights were a big deal. They setup a restaurant there for during the fights. People would get to know each other there, and it's like a company picnic; it's a company picnic where everyone has a gun. (laughs) The guy who ran the cockfighting barn liked me. He was always trying to get me to try different coke. He's always saying you gotta try this. And cockfighting was a big deal. It's no joke, it's like MMA for roosters. People go crazy for it. The Cuban guys I knew had these big houses in suburban areas. These houses looked normal, and one guy took me to one of his houses. This was one of the freakiest thing I've ever seen. The house was packed with little cages and roosters. These were mansions with nobody living in them but roosters.

"Boxing was a big thing too. In Miami there was a venue in the grove where we would go to these boxing matches. We hung out there with the Miami Dolphins head coach one time. This guy actually came over to me, Gilbert, and Pete—we were known thugs, we were known parts of whatever you want to call it—and he came over clear as day and he seemed to like us. He joked that half his players bought coke from us, but he was cool about it. The Colombian Mama went to that boxing place a lot too. She loved to gamble but, oh man, was she tough to look at in bright lights.

"You're from New York City, right?"

Connecticut.

"So you've seen those hot dog carts, right? Gilbert and his Cuban guys bought about twenty hot dog carts right around then. Those things are cheap, the hot dog carts. I remember them being kinda shocked at how inexpensive they were. Anyway, they bought about twenty hot dog carts, and they had them spread all around Miami, and for the people who knew, you could order a Cubano hot dog, which normally I think just has ham and maybe onions on top? Well, at these carts a Cubano hot dog meant big bags of coke.

"Heroin? It tended not to be a Cuban thing. One of my guys got into it big though because there was so much money to be made. It was shipped in wrecked cars on a car carrier from Miami to Greensboro. The driver of this car carrier did a bunch of coke and got all crazy at a motel with a bunch of hookers; he must've thought this shit was legal or something, that fucking idiot. The cops arrested him, seized his truck, and I don't think they knew what they had at first. But then somebody said something because then they found the heroin in those cars on that car carrier and that led to [redacted] getting clipped down in Miami."

Why do you keep mentioning Greensboro? Why was it central to your drug business?

Frank: "Because of its location on Interstate 85. It cuts into Virginia, it's a good hub location. Plus, there was a wrecking and car carrier business there that had connections to our guys in Miami."

Frank is showing me pictures of his girlfriend, Tammy, and him on vacation in exotic locales.

Frank: "I've always had hot women, and it's never about having a good line. It's not about being a pickup artist, it's about treating women nice. (laughs) Also, having a lot of money and cars and when I had backstage passes to the biggest bands in the world falling outta my pocket? Well, that was a time, and that didn't hurt either. But basically I've been the same way my whole life, I like to work out, and I like women. You see, Tammy is a very balanced person. She doesn't get scared easy. The girl that has my twins? She was one of my best drivers. If she got pulled over, the cop would just think, 'Hmm, she's real attractive.' They would put less effort into the check when it's a good-looking woman driving the car."

Did Tammy ever drive for you?

Frank: "I gotta think about that one. . . . No, not really. Let's say, if I needed something and I couldn't get it, she could go get it from somebody I knew. But she never drove a load, never. You know I got with her on her twenty-first birthday. I told you that, right? [No] Well, I'm sitting up in European Auto Clinic, and there comes this girl up in there, and I didn't know who she was. And she says, 'My husband sent me up here to talk to you.' And I said, 'Who's your husband?' Jimmy Whiting. She says, 'My husband needs to borrow five-thousand dollars to get out of jail.' I said that doesn't sound right, and there were guys up there with me. They were giving me the eye like, 'What's this about?' The story didn't sound right. So I go, 'Can't Jim's father (who's rich) give him the money?' She said no, he's been cut off. So I said, 'Alright.' Jimmy was a friend of mine, I gave her the money, and I said Jimmy would have to pay me back, no interest. So she said thanks, she understood, and she said what a shitty birthday she was having. I said, 'Hold on. What?' So I had one of my guy's run up the street and get her flowers, couple bottles of wine, food, champagne, all this other shit. So I kept her there, and I had all these gifts brought to her, and she was kinda blown away. She said, 'Well, this is the greatest thing ever.' I said, 'Well, if you want to see the best thing ever just give me a minute.' (laughs, leering) So I took her to Chic's Beach, and we relaxed and drank or whatnot and just hung out, and then after a couple hours we got wild, we got wild. And I told her Jimmy was a fuckup. He was constantly fucking up the smallest shit. So I told her Jimmy was never going to be nothing but trouble for her. So that's how that relationship started, from then on me and her kept a little thing going. Forty years now. Her parents back then were

— Rockstars and Executions —

a little concerned, like where are these cars and clothes and cash coming from? But we had a great time, we still do."

Day Ten

Kathleen

It's show and tell day. Kathleen shows me pictures of her family, her father playing guitar and violin, the arts store in Milwaukee, the community college library in Georgia, teaching courses on guitar. Lots of pictures of Kathleen hiking; she was a big hiker, she says. Her boyfriend wears a Women for Change t-shirt in one picture, and I ask if he wasn't dating her would he be wearing that t-shirt?

(laughs) "No. He was a cocky so-and-so. He was full of himself, and he wasn't afraid to play a role."

There are pictures of a march for Troy Davis. Pictures of Kathleen with Reverend Warnock.

"He's a senator now. He was very kind and very helpful during Troy's case. I talked to him nearly every single day during the Troy Anthony Davis protests; he helped people get there and back. As I look back, I'm happy and proud that I at least protested. If there was something I felt was wrong, I wasn't afraid to speak up and join in on calling bullshit."

The last thing she shows me is a book her father made for her just prior to his death.

— Rockstars and Executions —

"He wanted me to have everything he had learned. He wanted to keep it alive."

The book walks her through an endless parade of drawings, etchings, sketches, their family history, and history, period: descriptions of ancient Celtic cultures are found between drawings of Dolly Parton and Michelle Pfeiffer. Giuliani is etched between Milosevic and John Gotti.

"We would talk for hours, hours, and hours, then he would take me to Dairy Queen for an ice cream cone. Isn't it funny, the way we sometimes appreciate what we had only when it's gone, never to return?"

*****

Frank

"I did security for Jimi Hendrix at the Virginia Beach Dome. He had about nine hundred people there for his first show—not that many. This was way, way back in '66 or '67. He was the very first show I did. I didn't graduate high school until 1968."

Did he buy drugs from you?

"Well, I was so young, I didn't know anything about that then. Also, he's a black guy. So, you know, he wouldn't come to me for anything."

Really?

"Sure. Most times if I'm selling you drugs, you're white like me. People just, you know, tend to stick to themselves, to what they know."

Frank reads to me from a *The Virginian-Pilot* article about a Crosby, Stills, Nash & Young concert. 33,043 people, 67,000 Coca-Colas sold, 55 heat stroke, 9 drunks, 29 people needing bandages, 8 people with illness, and 27 people who had a little too much of certain illegal substances. Promoters hired 150 off-duty police officers. Four individuals were arrested for selling drugs.

Were you worried about off-duty cops or other security staff busting you at the shows?

"No. No way. It was just an understood thing. I had a Christmas party one year in Norfolk. (James) "Whitey" Durham, one of the biggest drug dealers in NC, was there, as were all my guys from Miami, all my group of guys. We had all these cars, man, Ferraris and Lamborghinis. So we had all these guys in a suite, and, so get this, I had hired a police officer I knew real well—he was related to a cousin of mine—as security for this Christmas party. Yea, you know, because I didn't want any of my people to go out, I wanted to be secure there. I didn't want nobody complaining. I didn't want nobody wanting to go drink and driving. I just felt comfortable with this one guy there. And hey, by the end of the night, he was as fucked-up as any of us.

"So I walked out onto the balcony with Whitey Durham, and I said, 'I want you to see how fucking crazy it is here in Norfolk with the cars, the way these things draw attention.' So I was standing there with Whitey and John, and I said, 'Watch this.' We were way up there, on a balcony way up there, and I threw a bottle into the bushes near the parking lot where all our Ferraris and Lambos were parked. The bottle smashed and about three cops came jumping out of the bushes, no fucking joke. They were watching the cars, waiting for us to leave, waiting to pull us over. That Christmas party was a bad idea. It's just a light story you know, but that was kind of the beginning of the end. All of a sudden, we couldn't buy security you could trust.

— Rockstars and Executions —

"The worst thing in the world is to leave a party and still be high on coke. There's no worse thing in the world than being behind the wheel with nowhere to go and that cocaine nervousness and that cocaine certainty setting in.

"Right around the time I did my second Jimi Hendrix show, I'd been in the business a little for a year by then. I did the Monkees. They were a big deal man. You know that was a TV show? They did a concert, and it was a different type of human being who came out to see them."

What do you mean?

"Well this is right around 1969. The Vietnam war is going and picking up steam, and the people who would come out for The Monkees were the anti-war type. The Virginia Beach Dome doesn't hold that many people; it's what I guess you'd call an intimate venue. And the ones who came there for The Monkees packed the place, and, holy shit, did they not like the idea of going to war."

Frank veers back to the topic of race and rock and roll unprompted.

"You should know, I was young—and this is naive to pretend one moment makes it all fine either way—but I remember I went and did a Stevie Wonder show. I think it was called the Portsmouth stadium; it was a baseball field. It was a big deal because it was Stevie Wonder. There wasn't much in the way of a stage. Anyway, I went to that show and I was the only white guy there, and it didn't make a difference. There were white guys who would tour with black acts and black guys who would tour with white acts, but it's rare, it's rare. People tend to stick to what they know.

"When it comes to selling drugs, I started with the marijuana, and I should've stuck with just that— marijuana and the hashish. But I couldn't have earned that tremendous amount of money like I did with the cocaine.

But looking back man, it's like going from drinking beers to drinking whiskey. It reaches that point, and ah, ah, ahhhh, you know?" He shakes his head. "I should've just stuck with the marijuana deals. Let me call Big O (name changed). He was one of the biggest drug dealers in the country. He was one of the last really big guys who operated out of Miami."

What does Big O do now?

"I can't tell you."

Does he live in this country?

"Fuck off, man!" (laughs)

Big O: "Frankie, that you, man?"

Frank: "Big O! Get this: I got this writer here, and he wants to hear my stories, you know? You cool with that? He's here now, and I got you on speaker."

Big O: "Shit, man, I don't know. What kind of stories?"

Frank: "Hey, man, let's call this—what do they call it?—fiction. We're just talking here."

Big O: "The fuck is the point of that, man? (laughs) Nah, I miss you, Frankie. How you been, man?"

Frank: "Oh, I'm good, man, I beat that cancer."

Big O: "That's good to hear, that's good to hear, man. So what did you want to talk about?"

Frank: "Did you take all the cars I shipped from Luxembourg?"

Big O: "I bought them all, yeah."

Frank: "I was living in Luxembourg at the time, and I was buying cars in Europe and shipping them, sometimes flying them, to Big O. I was the car connection for a little while."

Big O: "Porsches, Ferraris, and the AMGs from Austria."

Frank: "The dollar was different back then. I could make like ten grand on each car just because of the conversion to dollar."

Big O: "Those cars, man. Holy shit, they were beautiful."

Frank: "You see how with everything we did in the trafficking business, it's like one road, and all kinds of roads lead off it. Hey, do you remember that guy who I got the really nice car for and he painted it red?"

Big O: (laughs) "That was a fucking beautiful car, and he had it painted red. You were pissed!"

Frank: "You know he made *Time* magazine cover?"

Big O: "You also helped me get him that big body Mercedes, and the AMG with the special elephant skin interior."

Frank: "Didn't you keep at least one?"

Big O: "A Porsche 935."

Frank: "A fucking race car, and it was painted psychedelic."

Big O: "That was the car. I got a flat tire, and I went to grab the spare, and there were two kilos in the well. They weren't mine. I never found out where those came from."

Frank: "Hey, we're cool now. Are you cool with talking about your brother?"

Big O: "You met him at the rooster fights."

Frank: "He fucking loved cocaine."

Big O: "He would rooster fight and rip the heads off the roosters. The blood would be spewing everywhere. My brother had issues, you know."

Frank: "Remember what he did to that pig in Key West?"

Big O: "Yeah, they were pig fighting in some house in the Keys."

Frank: "I was scared of that motherfucker. He was a great guy though. Didn't we take him to the Playboy Club?"

Big O: "No, it wasn't the Playboy Club. We took him to that club; guys would be doing blow right there at the end of the bar, wide out in the open. Your Colombian Uncle showed up, and he was seriously about seventy, eighty years old, coked off his tits. Uncle snorted a toot right there in the open."

Frank: "Big O, I miss you, brother. I'm gonna come see you real soon."

Big O: "Frankie, take care man."

When they hang up I ask, "Cancer?" He deflects.

"Big O's brother killed a police sergeant. The police shot him up bad. He wasn't going to do no jail time after that. Big O did two federal bids. I think he's been locked up over a decade of his life."

Did someone like Big O resent you, someone who spent eight days of his life in jail?

"Shit no! No, he's happy for me. He was doing things and in places where there was no way to cover it. In my business, I would not go out of my little circle, but every fucking time I went out of my little circle I would get in trouble or it would go bad. I worked with a small circle. It's that debris out there, those little people that think they know and think they can help you or think they can hurt you; these little people are just debris, but they will fuck you up."

And there's no distrust even though you skated on your charges; they never thought you flipped?

"Shit no. I mean, maybe someone who don't know me might think that, but you just keep going. I had my small circle, and the big bosses, the bosses in Miami, were changing. Contacts are made over a lifetime, contacts and friends and family who know the way up and out. Hey, let me call Big O back. He needs to tell you about going blind in Las Vegas."

Frank: "Brother man, I meant to ask: Do you remember the time we went to Las Vegas?"

Big O: "I told you not to do it, but you fucking did it!"

Frank: "What happened was we were doing some work with an entertainment group in Las Vegas, and we were moving a lot of weight for the Cuban group through this Las Vegas entertainment union. So Big O's brother visited us while we were in Las Vegas doing a bit of work, and we had all this cocaine, and Big O's brother started breaking it out, and I don't know what was up, but the coke had been cut with something bad. And so Big O and someone else tried the coke and said, 'Fuck this. It's cut with something bad. Fuck this, don't do it.' But I figured I'm tough and we're having fun, so I tried a snort or two."

Big O: "Frankie was in the emergency room."

Frank: "We were in this hotel room, and I went fucking blind."

Big O: "A lot of meals on that trip were drinks instead of food."

Frank: "When you're up for a couple days like that you think the alcohol smooths you out."

Big O: "You were not very smoothed out that night."

Frank: "I couldn't see for a day. They put me in the hotel room and locked me in there. I remember looking at the water of the pool, and it was doing all sorts of stuff, and I'm thinking, 'Oh no, this is no good.' There's nothing worse than a bad drug trip. Alright Big O, talk to you later, brother.

"Gilbert Hernandez's father was a cab driver in Miami. He didn't need fares; he was a guy who dropped packages around town."

Did you and Gilbert Hernandez ever talk about the similarity in what your fathers were doing for work?

— Andrew Mallin —

"No. I don't know, maybe. Their father reminded me of Charles Bronson. He looked like he could kill anyone. He floated out of Cuba on a log. I don't know why, but he had to get out of Cuba 'cause of something. He finally got on a boat. He was scared because he was a wanted man in Cuba. He told us one night—he was fucking high out of his mind—but he told us what he told his sons: he killed the people on that boat. Some people were out on a boat and just fucking around, and they picked him up off his log, and once things had settled down he killed them and pitched their bodies overboard—and that's how he got to America.

"O.J. Simpson bought two kilos of coke from me at a Thomas Hearns fight in Las Vegas. He gave the female tennis player—she was a famous lesbian, Narvi-tuh-lova?"

Martina Navratilova?

"That's the one. You see, through the Coronado Connection we met a bunch of tennis people: Jimmy Connors and some other famous guys. Mike Agnar was involved with them, but that made a couple connections with new crowds. This is the Coronado Connection that *60 Minutes* was about. But there was a California guy who worked for Miami, and the California guy was moving serious weight in those days. He was the connection for a lot of these famous types, and so he just introduced me and O.J., and I liked football, so I already knew who he was. I wasn't introduced to the tennis player, but I watched him break off a couple ounces of one his kilos for her right there in front of me.

"I should tell you about The Sonesta. So all of us used to go to Sonesta beach. So you go over the bridge and over the Biscayne, and so after a big deal all of us would go over and calm down, you know what I mean? It's across the bridge and outside of Miami. There was a hamburger joint near the pool, and there was a Chinese food place, and I don't think we ever ate anything from either of those joints. But we would just get drinks after drinks, and we would just go wild. And so a guy we worked with, Bebito, had a condo there, a high end place; it wasn't supposed to be the kind of place where people like us are partying. And this motherfucker Bebito would take off, streaking in his underwear. He would just wear a bandanna around his head, and everyone was scared of this motherfucker. We had women there. We had the hot tub overflowing with women jumping in, and we'd be jumping in the pool naked before the sun comes up, and this is not a place where we can be doing any of this, but everyone with a pair of eyes is scared of Bebito, and so nobody is saying shit.

"He'd do crazy stuff like take a kilo up and smash it with his fist and break lines up with his fucking fist. And he had just had this hair transplant done. He was in his underwear, if anything, and he had this fucking bandanna on. He was the kind of guy who pulled his gun out quick. It's just, you know, fucking crazy."

So you would go there to celebrate?

"Yeah. You see, it's not easy to take it out of the boat or off of the truck. It's not easy. You've gotta spread it out, and you might have twenty guys working the thing, and you've got each of us with one eye on our part of the deal, but overall you're kinda worried too. That's the thing—the cocaine is so tricky, you understand that? Because people can overdrink, but if you overdo the cocaine, you die.

"They had these things called burn boxes. Well, after a while you learn how to look at cocaine and sniff it and figure out if that's the real deal. Those are still the best ways. But a burn box (lets) you turn up the heat, and it starts breaking down the powder, and the temperature at which the powder breaks down tells you everything about the quality of the content. When you heat it up you can turn the coke into crack. Like when you smell coffee, it smells kinda like that—different cuts smell like different things. There's shit like ether you can cut with, but you gotta know that different cuts smell like different cutting agents. If you cut with ether you had to combat the smell. There were certain products, like Mannitol, that were hard to get but were best to cut with.

"I only tried crack once and it was too fucking strong for me. It was not a good experience. I did not like that shit. I stopped messing with it because it can kill you, it deteriorates you real quick, especially if you go on a roll."

Roll?

"Yea, you know, like a two-day spin on it becomes four real quick. You do that and there's every chance you've got one foot in the grave. That's the thing, when I look back at my career, you could smoke all the weed in the world and you won't O.D. You might gain fifty pounds, but you won't overdose. (laughs) When you look at the prescription pills, the Quaaludes were the scariest because them bitches would knock you goofy. But there are other pills, and the cocaine and crack, and shit, man, it's scary. I feel like I saved lives by cutting my product with the big machete."

Machete?

"Machete is 'cut.' I would turn one key into two, cut it in half."

If I had showed up today with a big fat bag of cocaine and was like, let's blast off, would you get high?

"No. I just wouldn't."

"I have cancer, did I tell you that? No? Well, I was there in Ireland about a year ago, and I was having some trouble bleeding and stuff. I was training for another world's competition in powerlifting, and I was just bleeding a little, so I didn't think much of it. But I was bleeding more and more and more internally, so one day my cousin was going into town and says, 'You should come with me'—her husband died of cancer of her bladder—and she drove me to the doctor. I'm doing training, and my strength is going up, and they made me do the colonoscopy, and the doctor said I failed, and I was mad. I talked to him pissed off, so I said, 'Let's do one tomorrow.' So I drank that shit for the colonoscopy, and I had the worst hamstring pain of my life. I couldn't sleep, and I hit my head hard enough to fall over. I went out completely. I busted my face up bad. So when I went back the next day, I didn't tell him any of that, but after the colonoscopy, he said, 'I believe you have cancer, Frank.' It's like me looking at cars, after forty years he knew. So I went to the doctor who specialized in cancer, and he told me what I have to do. And I told him I feel strong and if I don't get this stuff done, what can happen? He said, 'You might last eight months, maybe a year, max.' I was bleeding so much I went from three pairs of underwear a day to wearing a pad to wearing a diaper, and even with the diaper I was leaving blood on the bench. I've never told another person that part of it until today. My son doesn't know that. I went through that.

"So, finally, I got treated in Wilmington, North Carolina. Chemo. I would go there for the radiation. I did thirty of them. I did thirty days. I was french-fried, brother, and I'm still feeling burnt by it. It's been going on one year and a couple months. That's where I was today, and why I'm so loopy today. I had to give blood, and they did the CAT scan. I'm good, but I don't like needles. That's why I'm a bit dopey today."

How's treatment going?

— Andrew Mallin —

"My health is perfect. They say once you have cancer you never get rid of it, that's what they say. But I'm training every day. They say a lot of people have cancer that don't even know they have cancer. But yeah man, I'm good. That'll make you look at life different, by the way, when someone says you have eight months left. [Levels a finger at me] You take things a bit more seriously. It was strange when I didn't take the chemo pills at first, but then each level of me cleaned up. Do it like a contest. After about three or four weeks of this, I felt clean. It messed with your energy, you know, when you're doing the treatment. I was short-stepping. You know short-stepping? I had no energy. That's the first time in my life I wasn't in the gym every day. I did not do any lifting once the treatment got serious. I would walk every day, but I didn't lift at all. Once those six weeks of treatment were done though, I was back in the gym, and I had been thinking about it, and I didn't just go back to bench, squat, and dead-lifting. I worked more stuff in, spent more hours each day stretching and testing myself mentally.

"I had one guy, he was a mailman with a truck. His route was in Portsmouth, Virginia. He was delivering pounds for me. I had about four-hundred, five-hundred pounds of marijuana stashed at that guy's house at one time! These were big bales too because I had sold some of it in bulk, so we had some fifty- to sixty-pound bales for some of it, and I was, like, 'Let's put this in your attic.' His girlfriend held the ladder for me while I did that, and I gave her five hundred bucks, and I started to walk off, and she said, 'I need to talk to you real quick.' And keep in mind, I never really talked to her before, but she was nervous and wanted to talk about Grady—that was this guy—and so she said, 'I need to tell you something.' And she clued me in that Grady was cutting my coke that I had stored with him.

Now, this is the woman who eventually shot herself in the DMV. She had two kids with me. She was attractive, and she drove for me. So when she told me about Grady, I set her up with her own place. My twins are about thirty-nine years old, that's how long ago it was."

What happened to Grady?

"I just distanced myself from him."

That's it?

"It's not like the movies; you don't kill everyone you come across or have a disagreement with. I mean, you can but you won't be around long. Mama (Griselda Blanco) was like that, but she was something else. No, that doesn't work with me. It's about keeping the business going. If he doesn't want to be in business, well then fuck him, but he might've been friends with someone, he might've had angels watching over him. It's just not worth it to me, not even then when I was a hothead sometimes. I put some distance in between me and him, and I moved her into her own place, set her up with a couple cars, had her driving for me."

Did he ever ask you what went wrong?

"No, I would just say things are changing, and I moved all my weed and shit out of his house. Never gave him another job. (laughs) No, I wasn't too worried about Grady or people like that because life is a little goofy, things happen. The other reason I wasn't worried was because Grady had introduced me to another mailman a while ago. This guy was black, and he was willing to work for me, so I reached out and that was that. I didn't really need Grady, and because I had his girl it was like, well, fuck him.

"The Quaalude king used to be a football player. I'll come up with his name; I try not to remember his name. He fucked me over, and then he tried acting like it was no big deal. His name was Biggs, that's his last name.

— **Andrew Mallin** —

"Less is best. Don't that make sense to you? And look, marijuana is like a firecracker—you get caught, you get slapped. Cocaine is a bomb. You don't want to be there when the bomb goes off. The cocaine business was basically a bunch of people playing hot potato. I mean, how are you going to make more money when you're in jail or dealing with lawyers? So when people come up to you in a rush and a huff and say, 'Hey man, can you get me ten keys in a hurry?', that's trouble waiting to happen. Take for example, I'm at a car show one time, and there's a guy I'm supposed to meet there because a friend of mine is asking me to meet him to maybe do some business. And this guy is telling me all about these cars and how the owner is a gangster who moves weight and how he and the guy are [holds two fingers up, intertwined]. Well, they were my fucking cars and my fucking car show! This fucking idiot is telling me he can't be trusted because he's willing to make up stupid shit like that."

How far and wide did what you sell reach?

"Luxembourg is pretty far away. Mostly, the weed and the coke went to New York, West Virginia, Tennessee, North Carolina, and of course, I was dealing it out of Florida and Virginia Beach, so a fair amount would go there. Boston, Mass., too. Some packages went up there from me, but that's it. It was never my thing but Portsmout. Virginia is famous for heroin. I had some wild friends there. I had one guy who I worked with, and he was selling heroin on the side. He got shot and killed. Fuck him."

Did you ever try to expand?

" No. See the places where I did business (were) because I had made connections through the rock and roll business. I did some business in Boston and West Virginia that was not directly connected to the rock and roll stuff, but you mostly could connect my business to people I met at the concerts or on the road.

"Well, actually, I remember, the place was Independence, Oregon. There was a guy there who was a pilot, and this guy had a connection to some trade coming from Southeast Asia—nothing to fuck with. The name of the town is Independence, and man, he had shit coming from Hawaii and Asia to there.

"Also, at one point, we came pretty close to setting up a legitimate business in Ecuador because we were going to use it to ship some more stuff through. So we were gonna do a yoga studio in Ecuador—as a front, you know? But it became too governmental, you know? That place is a bit different. The government guys didn't want cash and not to know, which is how things like that usually go down. No, these guys wanted the cash, and they did want to know the ins and outs. Didn't like that; the deal fell through."

Day Eleven

Kathleen

Frank: "I call it 'tossing you a thought.' Before you two start today, I told Kathleen, 'Think about the little girls around the world who were watching this girl who was a waitress in her spare time help wrongfully imprisoned men get out.' Kathleen's work changed people's lives. Think about that."

Kathleen: "Thanks, Frank."

"So after Roger Coleman's execution, I went to Israel for some vacation. Then, when I got home, I got a letter from a high school girl who said she didn't know women could be lawyers. Her dad said women aren't lawyers. I wrote back to her, and I offered her a recommendation letter. We traded letters for a while, then she went to college and got her first boyfriend, and I didn't hear from her again. (laughs) But what I did was go to elementary schools in the DC area and tell them about the death penalty work, and we talked about racism and confronting racism in their everyday life. They always asked one question, every time: how can you represent bad guys? I would answer that some of them are innocent. And we should not have a death penalty, period. The bad guys make the hardest cases but some of the most important ones."

Did you ever feel that your idealism was being taken advantage of?

"Um, I don't know. [long pause] You know, even if that was the case, I don't think I would care that much. The goal is still getting innocent people off death row and ensuring everyone is given a fair trial in this country. But no, I don't think I was taken advantage of, idealistic or not. However, there were a fair amount of people who came to me offering to help and who seemed to be in it for the wrong reason: they wanted to be famous. Usually, they'd say they have a lot of contacts, that they were gonna be good for my career or good for the person on death row."

Any other red flags?

"Well, yeah. They would ask for money. They would say stuff like that 'You're defending someone everyone else in this country thinks is guilty and you find them innocent, and that's remarkable . . . yadda yadda.' And I would say, 'I'm doing this for myself. I'm doing this pro bono.' You could taste what these people were after, though, by the tone of their voice. They wanted to sell me or sell the client, and they wanted to profit."

"After Roger's execution, Dustin Hoffman called me, and we started a conversation about the death penalty. That phone conversation lasted about a month. Eventually, he said, 'Kitty, can you come out to Brentwood and meet with me because I'd like to make a movie about you.' He and his wife and I went to dinner at Spago, and Dustin wanted to know about Roger's life, and I said sure. My law firm said 'no,' which didn't sit great with me because the point of the movie was to examine the sheer amount of evidence exculpating this man. They said, 'No, our corporate clients might see it and think we are grandstanding.' And I thought corporate clients had consciences too, and many of them don't believe in the death penalty.

"About Marc Rich, ninety percent of Giuliani's attack legally was that Marc was just a bad, rich guy. That's not a legal case! Rudy Giuliani was a well-respected tough ass, but one contact in the Southern District (of New York) said he crosses lines all the time, said they knew they were crossing lines under him but Giuliani had great corporate contacts. Bottom line though, as a person, I thought he was one of the most self-aggrandizing people I'd ever met. Aside from his friend, Trump, later in life.

"My father was a Republican, and I was a Republican. After I grew up a bit, I became a strict Libertarian. I became strict about it. I read several Libertarian texts."

Were you voting?

"All my life. I certainly didn't vote for Jimmy Carter. Clinton was the first Democrat I voted for, and I have been a Democrat since. And candidly, I voted for Clinton because of his wife. I was so impressed that he married a really smart woman, plus they had a Yale connection, and I was kinda cocky that way. (laughs) I didn't entirely like Hillary throughout her career, but I thought they would be good. I did not do local politics at all, and partly that was because it was a trap for conflicts of interest. Death penalty cases are minefields for conflict of interest, as are requests for clemency."

Is that book by your father your favorite family heirloom?

"A hundred percent, yes."

She won't discuss how bad her father's drinking problem was, or how much it impacted her early life.

"I went to Yugoslavia in college, Montenegro, to see if they could break away from Tito's government. We formed a model for companies about how they could self-sustain by doing workplace democracy.

— Rockstars and Executions —

Workplace democracy in Yugoslavia was the name of my senior thesis. I won a prize for best poli- sci thesis that year, and it paid for my trip to Yugoslavia. Sorry to brag.

"More people should know the difference between clemency and a pardon. Normally, an innocent person seeks a pardon. Although if you recall during Trump's era, he would talk about self-pardoning, and there would be this talk in the news about you can pardon someone who is not innocent."

You mentioned state laws being a roadblock?

"Some cases are dual-track. So what happens is you go through a state process, *coram nobis*—that's saying there was an error in a trial and you need to retrial. At the time, nobody had ever prevailed at this at the state level, but you were not allowed to advance the case to federal level until you had exhausted all state remedies.

"Take Roger Coleman, for example: he had some documents that had been submitted one day late and not considered. Basically, they thought Roger Coleman was innocent, but they hadn't sent anyone to investigate the original trial because the Plimpton guy was like, 'I'm not going to send my fancy New York boys down there; nobody will talk to them.' They said, 'Kitty, you're from the South. Do you want to work the investigation?'

"Roger Coleman's innocence was proven by his [redacted] [redacted]'s admission of guilt. This guy is still attacking women. He had a history of violence with knives back then, and I looked him up recently and he's got a record from the more recent past. Before Roger Coleman was executed, he asked me to try and keep an eye on the guy who did the crime. I forwarded evidence of [redacted]'s activities to prosecutors."

— Andrew Mallin —

*****

Frank

"I was the functional director of the [redacted] Medical Center. So I came up with a list I would do with each client, and they would do the half-hour or up to ninety-minute session with me. And everyone that came through me was sent for a sleep study, which the ladies at the front desk at [redacted] thought I was running a scam, but no, I lived there in the office, and we had six beds for sleep studies, which I think was the best thing I ever did.

"Hey Kitty! Kitty! Can you come back in here? [pause] Tell him about meeting me at [redacted]."

Kathleen: "Frank was a homeopathic care provider at [redacted], and they were interested in trying to get homeopathic care covered by Medicare for some of their patients. I was going to work with them when the strokes happened, and that was it for me. I went there as a patient, not as a lawyer."

Frank thanks her and she leaves.

Frank: "I would watch new patients walk from the doorway to the receptionist to me, and for me, that was hugely important to their care: how they're walking. I'm looking at their gait, how they walk, how they hold their head, are they smiling or do they look like they've just lost their best friend?

"So when I first started, I was diagnosing people before they'd even got next to me. It's a habit inherited from gangsterland, where you need to judge people quickly and stick to your gut. So after all the paperwork, I'd ask them two questions: what is the happiest you've ever been in your life? And I would ask them what was the saddest part of your life?

"Let me tell you, it was a showstopper, that saddest memory question. You would never believe what would happen when I said that. It was cathartic; it helped them talk about whatever it was that brought them there. The one that got me was this guy was playing golf, and he got hit by lightning. Everyone in a foursome got hit by lightning, and he was the only survivor. The lightning strike had destroyed his immune system. I would get them into strength training, yoga, meditation. The sleep studies and all that became the backing of a body of knowledge. This was the same time in my yoga we were beginning to work on astral travel yoga with Duke University-affiliated professionals. I called it' dimension leaping' to make it fun. That work was interesting and fun.

"What do you see when you close your eyes?"

Darkness.

"Well, in high meditation, the outside world disappears, and if you practice and practice, eat less, the blackness turns to fog and then the fogs starts dissipating and what happens is it turns white. In high yoga, we call this the 'white swan.' In some yoga pictures of old you'll see a swan on top of the head or a cobra fanned out over the head. Both of these refer to the white swan, and it will shock you. It'd be like you and me walking down the beach just talking and walking, and on the next step, you fall into a hole twenty feet deep—that kind of shock. If you can get to that place, you can see the elixir of life. It was so amazing watching that Duke kid leave their body. You know how you can tell someone has left their body and gone to a different dimension? Well, they'd just fall over. By the end of my time at [redacted], I learned to have pillows all around. That went on for years like that. I did that. Outside of [redacted], I was also doing martial arts, and through yoga I was teaching this famous rock climber. These are just stories that I wanted to share with you. You asked what kind of flipped me? Well, I kinda flipped in '99 when I went and lived in the Seychelles, and that's when life sort of flipped for me. There was a coup happening in Seychelles when I was there, and there were some guys following me when I was there, seeing if I was there fomenting trouble. But all I was doing was hiking up some hills and traveling in my body to other dimensions. You know, it's very expensive to live in the Seychelles. I made the news there because I was hiking the mountains, and I stayed up there for a night or two, maybe three, and I was dreaming and traveling, and I tell you brother, this isn't drug talk. This isn't some druggie talking, this is the journey of life stuff. And I was up in the mountains, and I didn't come back to my little hotel, and they sent police, and I was in the newspaper there, I remember. (laughs) They must've thought I was pretty crazy.

"Linda Hartwell died of a cocaine and alcohol overdose—don't print that. She was Bill Snouffer's girlfriend."

Why'd you just wink? You hook up?

"No. Well, yeah I did. This was when I had a couple cigarette boats, and I remember sleeping with Bill's wife on the cigarette boat. Bill was in jail. I remember we were hitting it there on the boat, and this horn went off, and I swear to god, I thought it was Bill. It was late at night, and they were blowing the horn on this big car ferry, and we're having sex, and I'm like, 'Is God yelling at me?' Nope, it's the ferry because we've drifted away from the fucking dock for some reason. We were just floating in the Norfolk channel. So the ferry gave us the horn big time, and it scared the shit outta me.

"The tour that Bill thought was going to be a big deal was the Beatles and John Cougar Mellencamp, but then George Harrison died. This is sometime around when I was staying with Linda Hartwell. Bill was crazy about Linda. He had been with his wife forever, and he and I share that good, old-fashioned Catholic guilt. So Bill was always trying to make it work with his wife even though he and Linda were crazy about each other. So I lived at Linda's, and Bill would visit all the time, and we were getting excited about doing this big reunion tour. Then George Harrison died.

"You wanted to know, after Big O was busting my balls, if we ever dressed like the guys on *Miami Vice*? They were dressing like me. (laughs) We watched that show a couple times. There were some people thinking about killing them. It was not good. That fucking show brought more heat on us drug dealers than a bunch of dead bodies or cargoes getting pinched."

Who was thinking of killing who?

"It wasn't me, but it was associates and friends in Miami, you follow me?"

Were the Hernandez brothers pissed?

"No, it was worse than that. The Colombian lady was not happy, and when Mama wasn't happy everyone got fucking scared. She was fucking pissed."

So who would they have killed?

"Well there's this guy, um, maybe he's a German guy? Well, he's the guy who made the show, and they were thinking about grabbing him, making him disappear. But things were so fucking crazy then. [Michael Mann is a German-American director and *Miami Vice* show creator.] She was so crazy, she sent people into malls to shoot the malls up if someone she wanted was in there. She sent people into Miami airport to shoot it up; she was not fucking around. She caused fucking trouble. She caused a lot of trouble. I mean, like I said, I would rather be Chinese than know about what she was up to."

I'd rather be Chinese? What that mean?

(sharp look) "You ever hear about them getting pinched? You ever read about Chinese guys getting pinched moving opium? No, you don't. So that's what I would say, I would say 'I'm going Chinese,' and my friends would know that meant I was going quiet, that they wouldn't be able to reach me for a time.

"I've been so many places I can't even remember. Looking at these pictures of Spain, and it's like, hold on, I was in Spain? That was that decade, man. I was a bad motherfucker. I remember going all over Sicily, Sardinia. I remember making friends there who wanted nothing more than to be in business with a guy from Miami. That's when I first kinda knew, hey man, this is bad. Miami was getting that reputation. It was too loud, it was too much. I started saying, 'Hey man, I'm from Virginia.'"

He keeps showing me pictures of his girlfriend, Tammy. He's very proud of her good looks. I ask why don't you marry her?

"She's the best, you know, but if I marry someone, I don't know if I could be a hundred percent with them, you know? And that wouldn't be fair."

So are you a hundred percent with her now?

"Uhhh, yeah.

"I wanted to tell you about Joe the Roar. I called him Joe the Roar. So Joe wanted me to train him, but he didn't come up to me. I have the reputation maybe for being a bit nutty, so his friends say, 'Hey, we didn't want to bother you, but there's this kid who is into lifting but he's really struggling.' So I met with Joe. He was a young black guy, and he couldn't hold onto the bar. It's all technique. So he's doing three hundred pounds easy, but his technique was not good. So I met him, and I charge a shitload of money for training [Eighteen-hundred a month got you three hours of training a day with Frank.] and he can't afford it. So I took him on."

As he's dialing, Frank looks at me and says that he really hopes Joe picks up.

Joe the Roar: "Sir! How are you?"

Frank: "Joe, good to hear your voice man. Hey, I'm with a writer, Andrew. Can you tell him how we met?"

Joe: "Hey Andrew. Well, Frank and I had a mutual acquaintance at Golds Gym on Battleground Ave in Greensboro. So one night a friend asked me if I knew Frank, and my friend says, 'Well, he's pretty impressive, so you'll meet him.' So I was at the gym one night like a week later, and we were there a little after midnight doing deadlifts. And we got to talking. I was looking for help with my training."

Frank: "Joe had the energy and drive, (but) he needed the guidance. Do you remember what I asked you before I agreed to train you?"

Joe: "Yeah. Andrew, I was raised by my grandparents. Frank asked what my living situation was, and I told Frank that, and he asked what would I do if someone messed with my grandmother? I said I would probably kill him."

Frank: "That's right. I agreed to start training you then."

Joe: "So Frank and I trained for three-to-five hours every morning. We'd wake up at midnight and go in and train 'til four or five in the morning. We did that for about four months; we were grinding pretty hard. Then he took me to my first contest, got me some exposure; it really changed my life. Not like I'm famous for lifting, (but) he gave me, you know, some appreciation of my purpose let's call it. I owe him many thanks for that."

Frank: "Can you tell him about your grandfather, and how he was killed?

Joe: "My grandfather was one of the first African-American police chiefs in America. He worked in a small town called Rich Square, North Carolina. It's the Woodland Police. My grandfather had been in the military. He was killed in the line of duty, July 16, 2000. He was actually shot. He had performed a routine traffic stop; someone ran a red light, he pulled the guy over, they were both ex-military and they talked about the military for a while, (and) then the guy bugged out and shot my grandfather."

Are you currently doing competitions? (We had just watched the video that gave Joe the Roar his name, the roar emanating from somewhere deep in his belly as he powered weight off the mat.)

Joe: "I'm not currently doing competitions, but I am just about to change jobs. My current job is crazy hours, but the new job is no overtime and when I'm in there I plan on getting back into power lifting competitions."

Frank: "You're gonna be a champion again in no time."

Joe: "Andrew, you can write this. When I met Frank, I was working and it was a crappy job, I was in graduate school, and I had hit a tough spot. I was working a dead-end job, and I owed a lot of money for school. I really needed some positive outlook and a good influence. At that point, I was kinda vulnerable. It could've gone either way. Like, I felt I had tried my best with grad school, but maybe it wasn't going to work out. And I had these, let's call them bad influences, trying to pull me in another direction. They had been friends, you know? It was a really tough time period. Frank was kind of a life saver."

— Rockstars and Executions —

Franks: "I remember we were driving back from a competition, and we were driving through Rocky Mountain, Virginia, and there were Confederate flags everywhere, and Joe says to me, 'Hey, can you speed up a little bit?' He pointed to all the flags. I said, 'You're with me, and we'll fuck up any of these racist motherfuckers.'" (laughs)

Joe: (laughs) "Hey, I gotta run. Nice to meet you, Andrew, and good to hear from you, Frank. Give me a call again anytime."

Frank: "You be good, Joe. Take care."

Does Joe know about your past?

"I had to be careful because at places like [redacted, medical treatment center that employed him] people didn't want to know that I'm a fucking smuggler. Nobody wants to know about grand jury indictments. That said, each person I trained, that's a new life. I get involved with the people I train. I try to help them. I knew how to make money too, so some people would look to me for that. But Joe, he just wanted help getting better at something he had set his mind to. He is a healthy, competitive person, and the one feeds the other."

Frank's cousin Gary Szymanski calls.

Frank: "Tell the story man about yourself."

Gary: "I worked for the Army Corps of Engineers for thirty-six years. I worked out of the Norfolk district. I couldn't join the service like I wanted because when I was eighteen my car got broadsided by a train going fifty-two miles per hour. The car popped like a bag of popcorn, and I got blown out the driver's-side door. I was in the hospital for ten months I remember Frankie and all my cousins visited me in the hospital, and I remember them giving me a suede jacket there at the Christmas in the hospital. His father was in the trucking business like my father was. It was a close-knit community."

Frank: "Tell him how you would bring Jacques Cousteau around to parties."

Gary: (laughs) "Well, I don't know about that. Do you remember his sailboat that had no sails? It was powered through wind, through like a wind thing, and he broke down in Hampton Roads. Our cousin Ricky worked at NOAA (National Oceanic and Atmospheric Administration). While Jacques Cousteau's boat was getting fixed, we spent some time with him, and yes, we brought him to a party you were having at the beach."

Frank: "Do you remember the time you helped me move the Porsches?"

Gary: "Have you ever seen the movie *Against All Odds*? It's a Porsche and a Ferrari racing through the streets, hell for leather; it's wild. Well, that movie reminds me of driving with Frankie that day. I vowed that day I'd never ride with Frankie again. We were going a hundred and five on the interstate."

Frank: "We drove those cars to one of my guys."

Gary: "I remember you had a Harley-Davidson that was all blacked-out, and you had 'Midnight Rider' on the gas tank. You boxed that policeman from across the street, you remember? That guy was seven feet tall. I remember all the guys from the neighborhood would come over to hang with Frankie, to jump rope and hit the bag."

Frank: "We were riding stolen motorcycles all over the place then. We had a good time. Pretty much all my cousins were pot smokers; some would take the Quaaludes, and I had to stop giving them around."

Gary: "When I got out of the hospital, Frankie would sometimes take me to a rock show he was working. He took me to Aerosmith; I was backstage. They had big trash bags full of ice and Budweiser. Steven Tyler was wearing, like, a referee's suit: it was black-and-white and shredded all up. That was the best concert I ever been to. That was 1978, and the Rolling Stones were coming to town, and Frankie offered me a ticket—as in, one ticket. So Frankie comes over and he's got forty-five tickets, and Frankie says, 'Just sell as many as you can.' I sold a whole pile of tickets. Linda Ronstadt, The Commodores, the people from the posters on my bedroom wall, and, I mean, here's my cousin telling me how much cocaine they do." (laughs)

They hang up.

Frank: "I don't even remember half of that. I was so fucking busy: t-shirts, cocaine, Quaaludes, rock shows. I do remember boxing that old cop; he was a tall son of a bitch. Seven foot might be stretching it. Gary was much younger than me. I was his big older cousin, you know? Gary only did cocaine once. I remember he didn't like it. He wouldn't ever do it again.

"I met Tony Bennett there at Waterside in Norfolk. This is where I had my cigarette boat docked, and the girl watching it would let me know if anyone was watching it because, you know, I kept stuff on that boat near all the time. I had little compartments. And I'm watching this guy walk this fucking dog, and he's dressed Italian mafioso: shoes high end, everything high end, and you can see he's got nice duds. I said to him, 'Mr. Bennett, you're one of my heroes.' And this is late in my career, so I think he was pretty damn old, and I don't think anyone else there knew who he was. His wife or girlfriend was drop-dead gorgeous—she was maybe like thirty tops and he was an old guy. Man, she was good-looking. He's still alive."

Frank shows me a picture of him surrounded by his weight-lifting trophies. His head is out a window and the trophies fill the lawn. I ask if he

— Andrew Mallin —

ever got trophies for yoga.

"Sure. Some of the trophies were blonde, and some of my yoga trophies were brunette. There were a few Asians, some more blondes. (laughs) Those are the kind of trophies you get doing yoga."

"You can bruise someone, you can slap them, fuck their girl—even that. But you stab them, shoot them? Nobody gets over it. It's a final act in more ways than one. So if you shoot someone, know that their people won't ever forget or forgive. Then you weld the door shut on that, you know?"

You mean forget it?

"Exactly. Forget it. But if you do have to do it, you tell yourself you're an archangel. I wouldn't do it just for kicks, like some I knew, because it is not a kick. It's not a kick at all. It's a weight. And the best thing to do is weld that door shut, weld it shut and never walk back through it. Forget it. You have to dissolve it quickly."

Frank, have you ever killed anyone?

[Camera pans from a crackling fire in the fireplace to a man perched in a high-backed chair.]

Hey kids, it's your Uncle Andrew here. For reasons such as legal exposure, we can't talk about the next couple pages of my notes. It is not in Frank's best legal interest to do so. I hope you can understand. Thank you for coming to my fireside chat, and please get off of Facebook. Love, hugs, and shoulder shrugs.

Day Twelve

Kathleen

Being a lawyer, were you a good liar?

"Yes. It's not something I'm proud of. So at my first job I was afraid to represent drug companies because prescription drugs hurt people, and I wouldn't work for (the firm's) biggest client, Phillip Morris. So they gave me American Red Cross as my first big client, so I figured I could represent them comfortably. I went in there, and I immediately started feeling guilty. They are averse to asking about people's sexuality; this was the time of AIDS, when gay and African-American people are being disproportionately affected. I knew that they were never once proven guilty in negligence (for) their care—nobody has Red Cross on the top of the list of organizations they would like to sue; it's not good press—but what they (Red Cross) did was create a settlement fund for the victims who had been ignored. I think it was two hundred million dollars, and that was like paying off the company's conscience I'm not saying the Red Cross is a bad organization—not at all—it was just my indoctrination into the reality that businesses are not ruled by what's right. That even good organizations can get hung up on social norms and pretending about, you know, what's staring them in the face."

You were born in Wisconsin?

"Waukesha, outside Milwaukee. My dad worked at an art store in downtown Milwaukee. We had six kids in the family. My dad and his brother Tommy were very tight. Tommy was an alcoholic, and Tommy had five kids of his own. So for a time we had eleven kids, so to speak. Mom and Dad were supporting all eleven kids. I had a fantastic childhood. My dad was supportive and gave us art to do. We moved to Arizona and he started selling cars, but he couldn't do much business in Arizona, and that's where we started starving."

What was your mom like through all this?

"Very angry."

Solely at him?

"Yeah. She had gone from a normal society wife—head of the symphony association, cocktails every day at 5 p.m., and bridge parties—to being a poor wife with six or eleven kids. Though I was not (pause) very close with her."

Arizona?

"My parents lost it. They were desperate. We were on our own. My oldest sister and brother would babysit kids, and that's how we would get money every so often to eat. We hung outside in the sun, and it was brutally hard. Hunger pains after not eating for three days are pretty terrible. The thing I remember is that after a couple days of not eating even a big drink of water is enough to make you cramp and throw up. Stone Mountain is not a very pretty place, but it was like a dream after Arizona. Mom got her job first, then she was able to get him a job, and he was good after that."

Do you want to talk about your road to recovery?

"I had my last drink in 2013. I saw these guys outside a church, and I asked them if they were AA. I'd been to a meeting before. They said, 'Yes, it's a meeting,' and Andrew, it was great. They were so supportive. What Frank is doing for me physically, mentally, emotionally, there are no words. The sun is the greatest thing in the world for my recovery. I'm still reading a book and a half a day. I've started getting into my art books. I love reading about the life stories of artists. Frank's cousin brought me acrylics and art supplies, so I'm excited to do some art. I'm going to do a series of blue sky circles with a darker blue surrounding and some yellows."

*****

Frank

"In trucking, bennies—Benzedrine—were called the Los Angeles Turnaround: as in, they'd keep you awake long enough to drive to Los Angeles and back. When my father was coming up, he had a Mack truck, and he was hooked up with some organized crime. It could've been liquor, it could've been cigarettes; he was hauling things. It was usually New York they were going to and from."

Do you want to talk about cancer?

"Yea, I can talk about it."

It's rare for Frank to be silent. Frank is silent for a decent chunk of time.

"Just . . . just let me clean off my glasses real quick. I'll be right back."

For the first time in our interviews, Frank excuses himself. He is gone for ten to fifteen minutes. When he returns, I say we don't have to talk about anything unless you . . .

"I'll talk about anything. Hey, when they brought me in, I was at a table with guys from U.S. Customs, IRS, DEA, FBI, and the ATF. All of them in a room, and I'm sitting there. So I did a little cocaine the night before the meeting, and they are grilling me, asking all kinds of questions, lots of questions about bodies, weapons, boats, the accusations about jewelry and artwork. And I just kept saying I need something to drink. I drank so much damn water in that meeting, and I was just peaking pretty hard because I hadn't slept the night before, not at all. I got dicked pretty good by U.S. Customs.

"Yeah I can talk about having cancer. I talked to my cousin about it, and she lied to me and said, 'Let's go somewhere,' and she took me straight to the doctor, and we did the colonoscopy. Pelvic floor cancer. Then I got the MRIs. Then I went for the thirty days, the sessions of radiation, the chemotherapy, the pills. There are so many doctors you gotta see, you know? It's like one introduces me to another, and you can't believe the number of people you have to work with just to get something done. So my doctor was Irish. I brought him a six-pack of Guinness 'cause I was hoping he could give me some good news. I brought in my most recent World's weightlifting trophy, and I showed it to him, and I said, 'I won this last year, and I want to win it next year,' so I said, 'If we need to do this, let's do this. I'll follow you a hundred percent.' I just wanted him to know I had a goal.

"After a couple weeks of radiation and the chemo, damn, things went so goofy. My diet flipped, my tastes flipped, I was so goofy. I got the COVID then too; things were not good. I lost maybe twenty-five to fifty

— Andrew Mallin —

percent of my strength in those weeks. That was the situation I was digging into when I got out of there. I was careful because I was a little fragile, you know? But the day I got out of there, I went and trained. I started that day. I got my strength back. I left in October for the World's. I went to the doctors before going to the World's. That's just going to be life from now on: every fucking time, gotta give blood, gotta get the CAT scan. But after chemo, that's the last pill I had to take. I don't like medication. I don't take any medication if I don't have to."

How did you do in those World's competitions?

"(Chest swells, jaw juts out) I finished first in four competitions. I got the medals and the plaques upstairs. I had dropped into the 158-162 weight range. It starts off with a squat, then a bench, then you finish with your dead lift. And this World's was in Virginia Beach, my hometown. My son came, a bunch of cousins and family came. One hundred fifty-eight: I hadn't weighed that since I was a freshman in high school. But I dug deep."

Is that your favorite competition?

"All of them were my favorite. Well, that one I felt the most accomplished. I had to dig deep. But this next one? I've been working even harder for this one coming up. I've had to change up to push myself. When I train someone, they win, you follow me? It's about doing your best and performing your best, and if you can do that, I accept that win or lose, you know what you mean? I'm not one of these assholes screaming about a loss. I'll take your fucking head off if you don't give me your all because that's what you owe yourself. Anything less, and you're just wasting the best part of you.

"You want to hear about The Beach Boys? I remember a time I was with Brian Wilson in Williamsburg, Virginia. They were all polite but really quiet, and, you know, until they got revved up on the drugs. Some of them went inwards and some of them went out on the drugs, you know? Talkative and outgoing. Dennis Wilson was always getting me in trouble. I mean, it wasn't an everyday thing, but like three times in my life I got yelled at for getting someone too fucked up on the drugs, and I think each of the three times was Dennis fucking Wilson. You could get burned out on tours though, you know? And they were a little singed. You know what it's like? It's like watching an athlete who is great and they have a couple injuries, and you're watching them wondering why they're not playing like they used to. What happens to an athlete when they get injured? Baseball, boxing, whatever, if they get hurt, and the injury might have all kinds of a diagnosis, you can track it, but it also leaks into their body in ways you can't track, do you understand what I'm saying? It's a depression, mental and physical. It bleeds over beyond the injury. Then you have a few different directions. Man up—if it's really bad and I can't perform, I'll go to the doctor and get the operation. That's an athlete. A rock star's doctor and operation is the drugs, you follow me? That's the kind of thing that you can't do forever; like an athlete, you can hit big numbers, but it comes at a cost. An athlete trains, can train their body; the cost of being famous and being a star is different.

"Something we're missing here, it came to me: what harm did I do my family by being in the drug business? The things like, 'Your father is a gangster, your father is a smuggler, he's a strong-arm guy.' They're saying this shit to my kids."

Did you ever talk to your kids about that kind of stuff?

"Well, not really." (sheepishly laughs)

"Brian Wilson, Williamsburg, Virginia. I pick them up at the airport and take them back to the hotel. So Brian says he needs to get some sleep, and we work out what time he wants me to wake him up. He says, 'Wake me up at one in the afternoon.' John was taking care of Dennis Wilson. We had four or five limos for Williamsburg. Brian was a little bit heavy then. So this is one p.m. We sit down at the bar at 1 p.m., and Brian orders a triple martini. I'm like, you gotta be fucking kidding me; this shit again? Immediately, that first order, it's like 'uh oh.'

"Steve Gudis was the guy who had hired John and me. He said, 'Please make sure he (Brian) shows up for the sound checks on the road.' Because Steve explained sound check was how they could see if Brian and Dennis were going to be, you know, among the living that day. Mike Love was the number-one singer in the band. He was doing all the singing heavy lifting. Brian and Dennis have to show up. They each needed separate limos, every member of the band, because they weren't getting on real good by then. So Steve Gudis—we had previous (history) with Brian and Dennis being a little wild—Steve was like, 'Whatever you do, do not sell them cocaine or pills, please.'

"So we're at the hotel bar, and he's starting with triple martinis at lunchtime. Brian? I can't even fucking believe he's still alive, and I just found out he's still touring. Crazy. Him and Ozzy Osbourne ought to do a show together, tour as the two guys who have no fucking business still being alive.

"After we got out of the bar, Brian Wilson wanted to go back up to his room, clean up a little, lay down. I said sound check is at five. He said, 'Fine, wake me up at four-forty-five.' Well, he wouldn't wake up. He finally woke up at six. He was not really happy. He did not want to be there. Well, Brian went to sound check, and he didn't do anything. He just acted all moody. And Mike Love came over, and Mike was the most businesslike guy. But more to the point, Mike always let it be known that the crowd seeing a good show mattered to him, it mattered a great deal. Whereas Brian was . . . well, Brian was about Brian. He would go to these sound checks and act like an asshole. He knew the songs, he wrote the fucking songs, whatever. He showed up and was pissed that he had to be there. So he left sound check, and he said, 'You know the area, let's go find a restaurant.' Food sounded like a good idea to me, get him ready for the show that night. But motherfucker, he was upset because what happened was I didn't have my briefcase on me; he wanted the drugs in my briefcase, he didn't want to get any food. We went back to the hotel, and I ran up and I grabbed my briefcase, and Brian Wilson is pointing at me across the parking lot, singing to me, yodeling. He was excited as shit. So we drove over to the hotel and then we went to Yorktown. We were in Williamsburg, the show was in a few hours, and the show was there in fucking Williamsburg. Yorktown is not around the corner! He was talking about the Revolutionary War, and he wanted to see something or other. We went to Yorktown, and as soon as I could, we high-tailed it back to the venue. I think we just about got there in time."

John Campbell worked The Beach Boys tour with Frank and returns Frank's call an hour after a discussion about not using John's real name. John is still touring with rock and roll acts.

John: "I've done about a thousand big shows, at least. You wanted to talk about The Beach Boys, Frankie? So we had The Beach Boys from Williamsburg to Johnson City, Tennessee. It was the old whole band there. I don't know who had died yet. I remember Mike Love was in charge already. I do remember Brian Wilson wearing that fur coat everywhere. We

— Andrew Mallin —

just did the service, it was the Williamsburg Hospitality House. They were flying private. We had to drop them at the airport and then head to Johnson City, Tennessee, but we went to that nightclub instead because Brian Wilson did not want to quit drinking for even a couple hours. And Andrew, at that time, Frank's biceps were twenty inches around. And I know because he would tell everyone, and I'm not a big guy, but we're in Johnson City, Tennessee, somewhere, and this guy is looking at Frank's arms, and he keeps talking shit to Frank, and this guy wants to arm wrestle Frank, and he was trying to be nice about it. And then this guy comes over and says, 'You're gonna have to show me something before you leave here tonight.' Brian Wilson was just enjoying the show, he was chill as can be. The guy weighed about three hundred pounds, and Frank lifted him off the ground, and I don't think Frank remembers because of whatever we were doing that night. (laughs) You know, we were on some of this and that, but I remember it clear as day: Frank lifted this guy off the ground by his throat and said real loud, 'I'm not doing any fucking arm wrestling tonight, but I will kick your ass.' I remember Brian Wilson thought that was the funniest thing ever.

"Kiss, Rolling Stones, Neil Diamond, any outside promoters would come in with the big bands, and I would put together whatever they needed: catering, and all their travel—Charlie Daniels, whoever—and so we got to knowing them. I left working for Frank in Virginia and moved to Tennessee. When I met my wife, I was the road manager of KC and The Sunshine Band."

Frank: "Are you cool talking about what you saw in Virginia?"

John: "I was not there in the same capacity as Mr. Sumner. (laughs) I went to work with Frank at European Auto Clinic, and there were some things going on, there were people interested in Mr. Sumner. I was in there one day (and) there's a glass atrium and there's two cars across the street. Frank said, 'You see those two cars? Those are federal agents.' Well, Frank had been sniffing cocaine, so I thought maybe he's being paranoid. But we have binoculars, and I picked them up, and I looked, and one of the agents was looking through his binoculars right back at me." (laughs)

Frank: "Assholes."

John: "So Frank says, 'If you take a car, one of them will follow you.' So I did, and I took a cop for a ride. He followed me the whole ride. I figured that was just about enough of working in Frank's shop for me."

Frank: "U.S. Customs Service. It wasn't even the cars, it was the boats that was getting the attention."

John: "I moved to Tennessee to work with Waylon Jennings—we did their lighting and sound—and I opened a limo service there. The World's Fair was coming to Knoxville in 1982. There was only one limo company in town. Company name started with a 'B,' so I named my limo company Ambassador so I was first in the yellow book. So I had all the Coca-Cola accounts. Steve Gudis and I were partners in that limo company; that's where the fallout started. Michael McDonald was staying with Steve during that World's Fair. When Frank showed up, he had a couple packages, and I remember Michael McDonald asked for a little bit, but Frank helped keep him clean—until finally, Frank gave him some drugs."

Frank: "Michael McDonald is a persuasive guy."

John: "Michael McDonald later hired me to production manage a show in Morgantown, West Virginia. They flew me out there. I had a helicopter to myself, a Bell 206B, that would land next to my Holiday Inn I was staying in and would take me out to this festival ground they were setting up. So the show was kinda falling apart. The two promoters were fucking with everyone, and they were trying to pay me in cocaine. I was enjoying myself with the helicopter. So they said all they could give me in terms of payment was a half-pound of cocaine."

Frank: "You wouldn't take that kinda payment today, would ya, brother?" (laughs)

John: "You're definitely not using my real name."

Frank: "KC and The Sunshine band were on tour in Thailand, and John was with them there too. Probably hung out with some cross-dressers, didn't you? Come on. (laughs) Hey, tell him about the time the KC and The Sunshine Band bird bit you."

John: "I was at KC's house, and his real name is Harry. I would call him Harry, or KC, or sometimes, depending who we're with, I'd call him Mr. KC. I had the opportunity to travel the world with him. We spent months in Asia together. Harry had a bunch of birds. I mean he had an atrium in his house. This one bird was red and blue. I want to call him a parakeet, but that makes him sound small, and this thing bit the shit out of me. So I walked up to this bird's atrium, and you can feed him nuts or whatever, and if you walk up to him without a nut he'll try to take your hand. So one day I'm sitting there on the couch. Harry was nice enough to extend his house to a couple of us, and this fucking bird is giving me the stink-eye. Harry would let 'em just walk around, Harry could handle them. Well this fucking bird just went for my knee. I swear, it was like that "Ride of the Valkyries" scene from *Apocalypse Now*. That fucker just swooped outta nowhere. Harry was a good guy, he didn't laugh too much at my misfortune. KC and The Sunshine Band had thirteen people in the backing band. They're a big act, literally. KC just did a show the other night, first show since the pandemic."

Frank: "John's company would bid, buy the rights to big acts that are coming through."

John: "Today, the business is much more regulated. Back then, we had road cases built to fit bottles of liquor. We had an entire road case built to store whiskey alone. Today, if you're drinking a beer on the job, with all the insurance and everything, you're gonna get fired. Back then, it was basically, 'Don't burn the stage down, and everything else is gravy.'"

Frank: "Alright, talk to you later, brother."

John: "You take care, Frankie."

Frank: "People took me seriously then because I was big and tough, but I could be conniving too. That's what wasn't on the surface. I say conniving, but maybe I'm just talking about being a businessman. And yeah, I know when you first met me you probably thought I'm all talk. But I'm real, man. I'm as real as they come.

"Rick James. You want to talk about an absolute fucking psycho? Rick James belonged in a mental hospital. That guy was a fucking handful. He could start a fight in an empty room. He was a piece of shit. Fuck that guy.

"It's an awful vice, I'm telling you, I know at least ten people that have lost their lives to cocaine, but the number of people who have had their life fall apart (because of) cocaine? Too many to count. And people now, I hear about it, they cut the cocaine with fucking fentanyl.

"The thing about Putin is he's probably been bullied. He's a small guy, and he's the kind of guy who remembers the insult. There are some kind of guys who love to remember that shit. Now he's been surrounded by 'yes' men so long, say, 'Yea, man, you are calm and collected on cocaine; it's no problem,' or say, 'Yea, man, you're nine feet tall, and your dick is measured with a yard stick, and the whole world is afraid of you.' That shit goes to your head."

My evening notes: Kathleen is tormented by the courts these days, barred from her own resources, living life as a gangster. Her crime? She had three strokes and a coma. The verdict? Hospital bills and tiptoeing away from personal bankruptcy. Frank ended lives, moved weight, put people in jails and hospitals, partied his ass off, chased everything in a skirt, and snorted coke like it was going out of style. (It has not) Today, he's a free man, able to rent a car, which for me still rings as one of the hallmarks of freedom and officialdom in America: the ability to rent a car—a car, the open American road and freedom—for money. Frank made friends with people who helped him traffic tons of marijuana and cocaine, as well as pills measured by gross weight because there were too many of the things. And he made some friends with the people who put him in jail for a meal or three for doing those things. Frank never had to try and recreate the *Goodfellas* prison scene, let alone any ode to *Shawshank*, because he was barely there long enough to hang a poster. You can sell drugs in America, just don't get sick in America. That's how you lose in America. That's on you.

Day Thirteen

Kathleen

"I had three strokes and a coma. After six weeks, I could see that white room that wasn't really there. Then a couple more weeks passed, and I asked a nurse—I totally forgot about this—I was in a hospital bed, and I asked the nurse to bring me alcohol. She said, 'I can't do that, and maybe when you get out of here you should think about going to rehab.' I said rehab was probably out of the picture as my law firm had cut me off their insurance; everything was on my own dime now and things were piling up. She was very nice. She even gave me her phone number and said before I try to get alcohol I should call her.

"The first AA meeting I ever went to was all men: about twenty guys, extremely supportive, and really human stories. It was like, 'Kitty, this is it. You're Irish, your father's Irish, this is in your blood.' I remember after that I felt like I was walking on water. I remembered thinking, looking at all these bottles I used to hide because I didn't want the neighbors to see the bottles in the garbage, I really didn't like the lying that came with alcoholism, and I thought, 'Look at these bottles, what a sad life.'

"My first therapist was a couples therapist. My boyfriend, Marc, had lost three jobs in quick succession, and I was supporting us, and he would yell at me to make dinner after a hard day's work. The therapist was like, you need to get out of this relationship and you need therapy because you've had a shit life."

Did you like her directness?

"I loved it. I like people who are candid. I would talk myself out of having had a shit life. I mean, everything in my life is still affected by starvation as a kid. I went to the restaurant with Frank the other day, I hid some tortilla chips. Why the fuck did I do that? I can't explain it, but it felt like a safety blanket. She recommended a therapist, and I went to him for three years, and he was the best. But I never once engaged with him about alcohol. I once told him I was drinking more than I wanted to, but I didn't engage with him on the topic. But I went through everything with him. We talked and talked, and we had a great time, and I had asked her when recommending a counselor for that person to be as direct as her—and he was. He said, 'You're not being fully honest with me. You're leaving things out.' But he also told me that the bargain I had made with myself—to work at the firm and do the work I want, pro bono, as a trade-off—he felt this deal, 'may not work out for me in the long term.' He was worried about my lupus. I had major lupus flares, and when it flared I couldn't clearly speak; my brain would feel swollen. People with lupus are more likely to have strokes, but it wasn't on my mind at the time."

Was having lupus tough?

"Yes, but I used it to my advantage too. Sometimes, my sores would be big and red and scaly. I mean they literally looked like someone with AIDS, so I could perceive (others) seeing me as having AIDS. So when I was in a deposition and I wanted to unsettle someone, if I had lupus sores

— Andrew Mallin —

I would let them see me. It looks like chicken pox but worse.

"I tell you, I feel I went month after month in tears, saying how can I not practice law? It's not the money, it's what I know how to do. People would call the firm and be told, 'She no longer works here.' I actually had a friend who picked me up and drove me all the way down to Alabama to tell a client that I could no longer defend him because I was no longer competent. For years, I could not remember what had happened the day before. I felt like people like my sister would call me up and say, 'I told you that yesterday, how can you not remember?' Not to bitch about it, but that's not real helpful.

"I don't remember the trip to Alabama. I've seen evidence of it. That was basically the end of my professional life, and I don't remember it. Then I got in touch with my friend Sylvia (Traymore) Pitt. She was someone I went to for help. She was a secretary at that time, and she went to all the other secretaries, and these people would call me out of the blue. Sylvia was a singer. She sang with Whitney Houston, she does impressions. She was just a kid starting out then, but she's kinda famous now, and to this day I email every single day with her. I tell her how I'm doing and ask about her travails and wonderful triumphs. Every day. Today, I'll tell her about the two walks to the beach I'm going to do.

"They would call me out of the blue, all these secretaries, and they would just talk to me. They would try to cheer me up, but sometimes we would just talk about the weather and, oh my goodness, that meant so much in those days. Those people, some of whom I barely knew, they saved my life I think. Now, how many partners from the firm that I had worked at for twenty years do you think called me? How many people with a law degree at that firm where I had given twenty years of my life, how many called?

— Rockstars and Executions —

Zero. It was the secretaries, the lowest-paid members of the firm, that reached out and helped me in my moment of need. I made partner after eight years, so I was a partner in the firm for sixteen years, and I made a very good income for them in addition to doing the pro bono work.

Did you have to push yourself to be an achiever?

"I loved it. It started with me reading a book a day. There was no way I was ever going to get a B. That's when I started pushing to go to college. I had to borrow money for the train ticket from Atlanta to New Haven—two hundred and twenty five dollars it was; I still remember that exact amount. I had to borrow the money for train fare, and I remember how long it took me to pay my high school teacher back. So the first thing at Yale was I couldn't afford the textbooks, but I had this one teacher there who told me about used books when I explained my situation. In college, I started drinking while working. I have the same problem—addiction—with sugar now.

"Monica Lewinsky asked me to represent her. I was in the know on DC politics in the Clinton era. I really enjoyed that. The strategies and the work didn't really make their way into the courtroom, the work was more networking.

"I remember my second year, and everyone was going home for Thanksgiving, and I said, 'Not only can I not afford a train ticket, but my friend Lane Whitney had invited to Maine.' They had a house there on the coast. This is the Whitney family, or at least part of it. Lane had gotten into Yale with absolutely zero challenge. She was a very pretty girl, and she smoked pot, which was totally new to me. My parents were upset I couldn't get down to Georgia, but Lane invited me to her family house, so it was good. The funny part was we were at this glorious house on the Maine coast, and this family is like American royalty, and my mom and dad had about twenty bucks between them. But they were having a nice thanksgiving meal at home while Mrs. Whitney served a canned ham for Thanksgiving. I'll never forget that! Everything was so fancy and so nice, and then something happened, and I guess she was pissed at Mr. Whitney about something, so she basically said, 'fuck it,' and said, 'You're all having a canned ham and you can go fuck yourselves.' None of this aloud; very polite, of course! And so Lane didn't even sit for the dinner. Me and her other friends sat for maybe thirty seconds, very awkward, then followed her away. I remember thinking (that) starving and living out of a station wagon maybe hadn't been so weird after all, that we all have these things we're dealing with."

Your three favorite films?

"*Gone With the Wind. The Godfather. A Few Good Men.*"

A book you'd want any stranger to read?

"*To Kill A Mockingbird*"

I read an article by Jake Tapper about you, Marc Rich, and Pincus Green. You represent a lot of guys named Pincus in your career?

"We represented him too. Pincus was the big family man, very different personality from Marc. He was everywhere, friends with everybody, lots of friends on Wall Street. Kind of useless as a resource, he was not the most intelligent guy ever, but where Marc was smart Pincus was the personality, the smooth operator. Marc was smart, but he was married to a suckwad—someone who uses others around them and does not give back."

*****

— Rockstars and Executions —

Frank

Frank comes into The Confessional ripping pissed. He is hot: Kitty has eaten a Reese's Peanut Butter Cup.

"I cook for her. I make sure she does not eat any processed food. I buy the vegetables. I buy the fruit. I go to the grocery store every morning. And it's not just that she's eating that food that is trying to kill her, it's that she lied about it. She only told me two days after eating the candy.

"I do not like liars. If you tell a lie in gangsterland, it fucks everything up. You need to be honest because what happens is when you have a guy in the business with you, you need the straight talk: Is the weight right? Is the money right? Have you double-checked? Is it taped? (Whether) it's marked (the kilo), (and) it's good to go. You have to say that you did the job, to not to leave any doubt. Because once you start working with someone and they say you're an ounce short, I know you're a liar and I won't have nothing to do with you anymore. Or, if you make a mistake you have to man up or woman up very quick. You resolve mistakes quick before they escalate, and you do it by coming clean. You lie, you better resolve things by being honest first and quickest—get it over with quick, like ripping a Band-Aid. Any kid knows that. And when you're dealing with lots of money, you need to deal with honest people. You're doing dishonest deeds—you have stolen cars, you have illegal shit fucking everywhere—but honesty is the most crucial thing in that business. It's no good for anyone when liars profit.

"Putin is like I said, a real Tom Cruise- and Prince-sized little fucker. He's got that little man syndrome, but he's gonna get popped. They're going to take his ass out because the guys that don't like him are around him.

— Andrew Mallin —

They're right around him.

"Two guys tried to kill me in my condo at Chic's Beach. I had a condo in Virginia Beach, and people would come up there to try and contact me for the business. Something happened with these two guys that I can't talk about, and they lost a bunch of money on a deal, so they were in a pinch. They contacted me and were coming out to my condo, not about money but about another deal, you know? They had some packages of cocaine and some jewelry, so I looked at it and I'm like, 'Nah, I don't really need that.' The coke wasn't even great quality; these guys are wasting my time. And I'm talking to the guy who does the talking for his idiot friend, and his eyes go all sideways like he's looking at something behind me. His friend had got behind me, he was trying to choke me, and I backed him up and rammed him into the corner of this fish tank. I had a huge fish tank filled with tropical fish, and this thing was in the middle of the room. I pushed back and dropped the back of his head right on the corner of that tank. Boom, glass everywhere, fish flopping around. I kicked the shit out of his friend while the other guy had the fish tank corner in his head. I kicked him and stomped him . . ."

[Camera pans from a crackling fire in the fireplace to a man in a high-backed chair.]

Hey kids, it's your Uncle Andrew here again. We can't talk about the next couple pages of my notes as it is not in Frank's legal interest to do so, and nobody ever died with their skull caved in on a fish tank. I appreciate your understanding that this was not the case. Drive safe and remember, always wear a seatbelt. Peace, love and belt buckle to belt buckle hugs.

Frank has his phone out. He's calling Bill Snouffer's widow, Sue.

"Hey Sue, it's Hammer. I got the writer guy here. Are you cool to talk about Bill and the tours he was on and how you met me? Is that cool?"

Sue Snouffer: "I guess."

Frank: "This is a helpful thing, you feel me? So you just go."

Sue: "Well, Bill got into the rock and roll from martial arts. He'd always been into martial arts. He and I met in the seventh grade. When the rock and roll thing took off for Bill, it was because Steve Gudis, who was a big, big promoter, was looking for someone with martial arts to do security at the Greensboro Coliseum. From there, (Bill) got on tours. Whenever he was gone on tour he had someone working for him, holding down security at the Coliseum. This is the Greensboro Coliseum, of course.

"I met Frankie when we were twenty-four or twenty-five. It was in Greensboro. Bill brought Frankie to our house. They were both into rock and roll and security and martial arts. Bill and Frank were like brothers. Yes, I did like Frank from the beginning. He's got a very big personality.

"Bill liked Billy Joel a lot. He liked Ozzy Osbourne too. Ozzy came to our house one time. He came to pick up Bill one time to go eat Japanese food. We had no clue he was coming over before he rang the doorbell. Open the front door, and it was Ozzy Osbourne with a huge smile on his face saying, 'Is Bill there and is he hungry for sushi?' Bill loved sushi and crazy Indian food.

"Billy Joel, yes. I flew up to New York one time when they were all up there in Long Island. Billy Joel was putting on a show, maybe at Jones Beach? They gave me a limo driver for the day because I had no idea where to go. The limo drove all around New York City with the driver pointing out the sights. After the show that night, we all went back to Billy Joel's house and partied. Billy lived in Oyster Bay, New York, in what they called 'The Glass House.' Billy Joel had a white German shepherd dog. Never seen anything like that dog. I remember Billy was really proud of that dog. It was just really nice meeting all those people. Richie Cannata played the sax for Billy Joel. Bill and I went to his wedding in New York. Liberty (Devitto), Billy Joel's drummer—his wife was from the same town as my parents: Clinton, New Jersey. We all got along fine.

"One of Bill's first tours was with ELO, Electric Light Orchestra. They were doing a show in New York City, and I met them there. We all went to Studio 54. The place was packed. I didn't really spend any time with ELO band members. It was fun, but, well, you know, I just felt out of place. I've never seen anything quite like Studio 54."

Frank: "But Bill and I brought you out in Miami a bunch, right? That wasn't that much different."

Sue: "I remember Bill was doing Bob Seger down in Miami. I met you both after that. We went down to the Coconut Grove. Orlando was where you guys did The Rolling Stones; that was pretty wild. I remember the Billy Joel show in Miami. We had that police escort, and we were in-between the highway patrol and a huge crowd, in the limousine, and they were just going crazy. The people in the limousine were going kinda crazy too, but, you know". (laughs)

Frank: "Remember going to California?"

Sue: "San Francisco. That was the Prince tour. Bill was supposed to have a break, but Prince wanted him on tour. Even when I was in San Fran with you all we didn't see a whole lot of Bill,. although we did go to wine country and Alcatraz."

Frank: "Bill and I did not enjoy visiting Alcatraz."

Is it tough to talk about rock and roll?

Sue: "Yes. It's a good time that went bad."

— Rockstars and Executions —

Do you want to talk about that?

Sue: "No, not really."

Frank: "Hey, do you remember them crazy outfits Hobart would wear? Hobart was Bill's secretary. Bill had an office in Greensboro. There were pictures of him with rock stars all over the place there. The first (time) I visited Bill Snouffer, there this guy comes up to me in like a blue chiffon, like a silk robe, and I asked Bill, 'What the fuck is this?' And Bill introduced us, he said, 'This is Hobart. You've been talking to him on the phone for a year.' And this Hobart, in a singsong, was like, 'They call you Hammer, and I wanted to meet me the Hammer.'"

Sue: "Hobart was gay, but he liked straight men. He was a hoot."

Frank: "One of the funniest guys I ever met. I remember one time Hobart thought espresso shots were cocaine. We were in a hotel or something in Miami, and he thought the waiters were serving cocaine. It was espressos."

Sue: "We were with Steve Gudis."

Frank: "That's right. Hey, when was Bill in jail?"

Sue: "Bill went in in 1985, and he didn't get out of jail until 1992."

Frank: "That's right, 1985 is when he got arrested. Bill's lawyer tried to put me in jail, but that's neither here nor there. From jail Bill gave me a coded message to dig under his mother's house. He was on a jailhouse phone call so he couldn't talk plain, and it took a while, but I understood what he was saying eventually. I drove to his mother's house with a shovel. It was the middle of the night. It was a dirt floor crawl space under his mother's front porch, and I was in there in my nice clothes. I was dirty as hell, and I got the scare of my life."

Sue: "Helen was up?"

Frank: "His fucking mother was awake! I was in this crawlspace, covered in dirt, digging everywhere I can think, and when I look up, his mother was there beside me in her nightgown. I nearly ran. And what was she doing?"

Sue: "Was Helen praying up a storm?"

Frank: "While I was digging, she was praying! I dug eighty-two-thousand dollars out of there with a cracked shovel. And when I hit the money, I'll always remember this, Bill Snouffer's mother was saying over and over again, pretty loud too, 'Thank you Jesus.' That was one of Bill's stashes, but do you remember the heated teepee?" (laughs)

Sue: (laughing) "Oh my goodness!"

Frank: "Bill had this teepee with a heater in it. Anyway, he was convinced he had hidden money under that thing. When he got out, he dug up every inch of ground under where it had been."

Sue: (laughing) "He eventually brought in someone with a backhoe." (laughs)

Frank: "Well, me and him were pretty crazy then, right? Did he ever find anything there?"

Sue: "No."

Frank: "Take care of yourself, Miss Sue. (laughs) I'm gonna come visit you. You put on a mini skirt, and I'll come down and take you out."

Sue: (laughs) "Alright, sounds good. Love you, Frankie."

Frank: "Doctor Pie was one of Bill Snouffer's martial arts teachers. Doctor Pie was based out of Florida. He was really into martial arts, and he was really into lifting weights. He was a seventh- or eighth-degree black belt. Doctor Pie had provided security for Elvis Presley for many years. Doctor Pie had gone on tour a little bit in his life, but he did not like to tour.

— Rockstars and Executions —

I worked with him once; he met us in Orlando to do a Rolling Stones show. Doc Pie did that one as a special favor to Bill, who needed help that night. Doctor Pie, I think he was Hawaiian. Elvis Presley was a big-time martial arts guy. He was not a real battler, he's more of a stance guy. I did a couple Elvis shows, and he would do a martial arts warm-up.

"Same for Van Halen, what, twenty years later, David Lee Roth and Elvis would warm up by doing kicking. Elvis warming up singing "Kung Fu Fighting" was one of the funniest things I've ever seen. Mick Jagger did a lot of stretching before shows.

"No, Doctor Pie was not into the drugs. The guys giving Elvis drugs all went through the Colonel (Tom Parker); they had to. With me and Bill, it was kilos and kilos. We were in the rock and roll business, and that's what the bands wanted. And the majority of people in this world don't know what real cocaine is. They know what stuff that's been cut a bunch is like, and that's wild enough. The bands got the real stuff, and it's hard not to get fried on that.

"Bill Snouffer did the same thing to his nose that Stevie Nicks did: he burned a hole through it. You would see the guys who had gotten the cocaine thing bad. They would either have Vaseline under their nose, or they'd have the little beard on their upper lip and the beard would be burned, the skin would be cracked and inflamed."

What's that from?

"That's where the cocaine would leak out, you know, and burn. That's what that's from."

"Every taxi driver I ever had in New York City was on cocaine. I'm not joking. I'm not telling you they were driving fast, I am telling you they did cocaine. Waiters, waitresses, concierge, you name it; there was a time in this country when everyone was either selling it or doing cocaine themselves."

I believe that is called "projecting," sir.

"I was with Customs and some FBI guys; I was working with them at that point. Two guys came from Luxembourg to buy a bunch of kilos of cocaine. These two guys had a stewardess acquaintance who would be able to fly the cocaine back. This deal was sending cocaine to Reykjavik and to Luxembourg. My government nickname was Don Juan—'cause of the cocaine and girls. I know you're laughing, but that's in my folder at U.S. Customs. Ozzy showed it to me. So I gotta do this deal with the Europeans, and I'm wearing the listening thing. We go to this fancy restaurant in Virginia Beach, and we're ordering food, and there are guys outside sitting in their cars—recording devices on us, they're recording everything we're saying.

"I remember that was the night the *maître d'* comes over, and he was just being casual, he was just being normal. He goes, 'Frankie, you got any fucking cocaine on you? I could sure use some.' And I just said, 'Ummm, I'm gonna have to talk to you about that later.' I was wire tapped all from my balls to my chest. The two agents I was sitting having the meal with were kinda laughing, kinda pissed. They wanted to know, 'What the fuck was that all about?' We had to wait a while for the other guys to show, and they were getting kinda pissy with me.

"After the Prince tour, Bill left a note on Sue's bed saying, "I gotta go see Frank. I'll be outta the country"—'cause I was in Luxembourg. When he told me that, I thought it was the craziest thing ever, like he didn't want to have a minute-long conversation at least? So Bill came to see me."

What happened?

"We got nuttier than a fruit cake. He had said when the Prince tour was over he was going to come see me because he needed a break. Well, a break meant we were gonna be doing all the cocaine. We were going out all the time, all night long. We started, we were rolling, and we were crazy as motherfuckers. We partied with my guy Alex—his family owns CargoLux. We had met Alex on the Prince tour, and he had partied in Miami with Prince and Michael Jackson because we had made those introductions. Alex Gross liked that shit.

"I took Bill to Cannes, France—that's the French Riviera. We had a captain we were giving a lot of money to everyday, he drove the boat and took us diving to a bunch of crazy spots. At that point, the girl, Marion, that I was living with in Luxembourg had about enough of Bill and me, so I told her to drive home to Luxembourg. Bill and I went to Rome. Crazy wild. We went to the Excelsior Hotel in Rome. Bars, all that stuff. We met some punks who thought they were bad fucking motherfuckers. Him and I started rocking and rolling. When the fight was over, we went somewhere else. I don't remember, but it was a fun time. I remember Bill had a lot of blood on one arm and none of it was his, cuts to the face, and (his) nose just (bled) a lot.

"When I got back to Luxembourg, I did threaten to throw Marion into the pond out back of the house her and I were sharing. See, I had told Marion we were going to get crazy, and we got crazy, so what was the big surprise? I knew I shouldn't have said that though. Police showed up, and they escorted us out of Luxembourg. I had to leave a bunch of my shit at Marion's place in Luxembourg. They escorted us to the border of France and Germany and told us not to come back. We flew home from . . . I don't even remember; we were burnt-up. I think Alex Gross took us to the

Frankfurt airport. Yes, that's what it was."

Frank shows me the picture of being arrested in Virginia Beach. The Frank Sumner in the picture is very different-looking from the slender hard man whose face is all planes and angles who sits in front of me. The Frank Sumner in the picture is fucking huge, for one: his arms are legitimately, startlingly large. And he is not handcuffed. One police officer with his back to the person taking the photo opens the rear door. "Virginia Beach Police" is visible on the car door. In the background, three or four other patrol cars have their doors open and lights on. A black officer in sunglasses is pointing at whoever is taking the picture, yelling at them, while around him a bunch of white officers look at the ground or elsewhere.

His girlfriend took the picture while Frank was being arrested. Her name is Kathleen Hudson, a triathlete.

"What is it with all the Kathleens that have been in my life?"

"When the guys arrested me that day, they didn't handcuff me. I went quiet.

"Going way, way back, Steve Gudis met me in Virginia Beach, and Bill Snouffer in Greensboro, North Carolina. Bill Snouffer was introduced to me as 'the white dragon.' He was mostly into kung fu. It says that on his gravestone: the white dragon. Bill was the guy who taught me to carry the drugs in a briefcase at the rock shows, to keep it cool.

"I kept bringing the briefcase full of drugs even during the shows. Onstage, with lights and cameras on the stage, and there's me and my briefcase. After Bill got busted, I looked back and thought, 'Oh my God, they're gonna come back and get me.' Whitey Durham knew all about it. I said, 'I'm the fuck outta here, out of the country.'"

Quickfire question time: Edgar and Johnny Winter?

— Rockstars and Executions —

"Nice guys. They wore big cowboy hats, and they were pink albinos. They had crazy sensitivity to light. I don't just mean sunlight. I mean they, well, their eyes could not adjust. I was trying to bring Johnny on stage one night (laughs) and someone says, 'Hey Hammer,' and I looked to see who it was, and, well, Johnny Winter cannot see well at all, and I was being an idiot trying to see who was talking to me, and I walked him right into the wall. (laughs) I was trying to just see who it was and Johnny couldn't see shit. But after bumping him into the wall, he was fine. Him and his brother were very cool."

Rick James?

"Wild, fucking awful. Cocaine, women—it didn't matter to him; he was dialed in to another fucking channel from the rest of us."

Why won't you be more specific?

"Because I am trying very fucking hard to block any memory of Rick James."

Motley Crue?

"They wanted me to go on tour with them, but I was doing other things then. I had Tommy Lee at the Volunteer Jam in Nashville. Tommy Lee asked me would I want to go on tour with them. We were doing cocaine, and Tommy was looking at my arms. He wanted me to go on tour with them. I said no, but I said I'd meet him anywhere with cocaine.

KISS?

"Gene Simmons and KISS—if you want to talk about oddballs, there you go. Just because of how many hours a day it was to get them in and out of makeup, it just wasn't my deal. Actually (my girlfriend) Tammy cut Gene Simmons' hair before a concert one time. He was in a panic, and so Tammy came there as a special favor, and Gene Simmons was a rude asshole to her. I'll have to ask Tammy about that, but I remember him being a rude asshole, and she was doing him a favor. He's saying, 'No, you cut my hair like my guy always does it.' I had half a mind to pop Gene Simmons a couple times that day."

Joe Cocker?

"Oh, great one. I did five or six shows. He was very intense. He looked like he was eighty years old when he was thirty five. He had so many quirks, so many little hand gestures. Top shelf entertainer, he had to work for it. He had a group behind him that was powerful, and they picked up a lot of the energy."

Bruce Springsteen?

"I liked him because in his warm-ups he would say stuff like, 'Damn, the jeans are tight tonight!' And he would kind of make fun of himself, you know? Before he got real famous, his singing was harder to understand, that make sense? Once he got bigger, he started singing a little clearer at his shows. Bruce was a cool guy, though. He had a lot of energy, and he didn't do any cocaine. He suffered from depression. I never saw him do cocaine. I can't say he didn't do cocaine, but I never saw him do cocaine. He was more of a thoughtful guy. He was good. He was nice too. He wasn't afraid to laugh at himself."

Phil Collins?

"Phil Collins is surprisingly shy. I was doing Genesis shows; he wasn't a solo act yet then. Not rude at all, really nice guy, and he had a good touring group with him. His road crew was good, and they all got along. I've heard lately things all fell apart for him, like his road crew and them told him to fuck off after a while. You see him now, and it looks like he's got the cancer. Back when he did a tour with a guy called Billy Ocean, that was a wild tour. Lot of partying on that tour."

Neil Diamond?

"A crooner and a singer who appeals to a certain demographic only. Jewish men and women loved him. His crowds, even when he was a young guy, his crowds were old. He reminds me of that guy (Engelbert) Humperdinck; you remember that Humperdinck? It was Humperdinck, Tom Jones, and Neil Diamond; they were about of the same status. They would do concerts, but it was not a rock and roll show, do you know what I mean? Ballads and stuff like that, you know, boring shit."

Jimmy Buffett?

"I did lots of his shows. He was laid-back like you'd probably expect. Mostly, he would do college venues. I did him at (the College of) William & Mary a couple times. He would always try to do outdoor venues if he could. He was big at a certain time, but other times his concerts would be kinda depressing, you know? You get tired of being around that same kind of music. I don't know. I've seen some old rock and rollers put on shows where they no longer had a fastball of any kind, but those shows weren't depressing the way some of Jimmy Buffett's shows felt depressing."

Barry White?

"He would call me at home when he was around. You ever (hear) Barry White's voice over the phone? I can't even try. Anyway he'd say, 'Hey, Hammer. Come and see me at the Coliseum, 'cause I'm here.' That's about all the conversation he and I would ever have. He liked the weed too, but I know what he meant. He loved cocaine. The Commodores liked weed too, especially Lionel Richie. But that's nothing compared to what Barry White was doing. He loved cocaine."

Stevie Wonder?

"A different type of guy on stage. He could sing. He played the harmonica. He could put on all kinds of shows. Stevie, he only had Black people around him. It was on the fringe of . . . I mean . . . that was when . . . I mean . . . because of when . . . I mean . . . things were fucking segregated back then. (long pause) Exactly. It was not a good time to be a Black man in America."

Jimi Hendrix?

"He almost looked sick the second time I saw him—kind of a different concert. It was not a powerful concert the first time, does that make sense? That was at the Virginia Beach Dome. His first show he wasn't that powerful in concert. The second one of his he fucking had power out the ass. He pretty much melted his guitar, but he did not look very well. He had put a lot of wear on his body in less than a year. I don't know, I thought he looked sick. I was so fucking young though, I probably wouldn't have looked at him twice in the early '80s. He would've fit in fine with all of us then. You see the rings and darkness under my eyes in that picture of me getting arrested at my girlfriend's? None of us were sleeping; none of us looked healthy."

Elton John?

"He would talk about soccer all the time, and I didn't even know what soccer was. He was pretty much obsessed with soccer. He was into his wardrobe and being flawless. He took a liking to Hobart, who was a gay guy who did all the stage stuff, and Hobart was very, very particular. He did things right, and so Elton John and Hobart got on real good. They were both perfectionists. Elton's room had to be right, Elton's backstage had to be right, the food backstage had to be right. Elton was a perfectionist, but he wasn't some asshole running around yelling that things aren't right.

Elton was there hours before the show, helping make sure things are the way things are supposed to be. He was a help rather than a hindrance. And on tour, Billy Joel was a bit more in his own world, drugs and whatnot. Billy Joel loved scotch and cocaine. I think Elton might have been stone sober on that tour. Either way, I didn't sell him anything. I didn't see him do anything, and my eyes are sharp. Elton John is someone I would say I have a great deal of respect for."

Dolly Parton?

"I walked her on stage a couple times. She's not my style because she is so made-up. The wig is fake, the eye things are fake, and here's the weird thing—Dolly had a woman who took care of her and helped with the wigs and everything; well, that woman looked exactly like Dolly Parton too, which was kinda weird, you know? Dolly could sing, but she did not move around the stage at all. Her shows were more just her standing there belting it out."

Tina Turner?

"Tina Turner was the best female performer I've ever seen, for fucking sure. She was all for it. She filled the room with energy. She reminded me, and this is going to sound fucking weird, but she and Alice Cooper are in the same place in my memory. They were there to put on a fucking great show."

Sting?

"I did several of his shows, and honestly, I couldn't tell you a thing about them. I do know he did a song with the Dire Straits. He was at a show, and he played their song, and it brought the fucking house down—that MTV song. If you listen, that's Sting on there—"I want my MTV"—that's Sting. Dire Straits were who I listened to the most when I was in

India for those years. I loved Dire Straits."

Kenny Loggins?

"Great fucking shows. Him and Loggins and Messina. (Jim) Messina was in Poco later. Kenny Loggins was an animal for women. He had a lot of fine-looking women around him."

Bob Dylan?

"I don't think he liked me. He was touring with Joan Baez in Europe; it did not go well. They had a thing going for each other since forever, Dylan and Joan Baez. Bob was a very nice guy but he was strange."

The number one entertainer of all time?

"I would put my money on one guy. If it was a contest between all the bands ever and they were all at their best; if you put all of them together and all of them were at their very, very best, and you watch James Brown when he was dancing and moving and putting on a show, this guy took it (to) another level. James Brown in his prime was better than Elvis in his prime. And we're talking about a very handsome white guy versus a pretty ugly black guy. But at the end of the day, James Brown was such a dancing fool and such a good singer, yes, I think he was the best ever."

When I say music legend, who is the first person you think of?

"Elvis Presley."

When I say that a musician never got the respect they deserved, who do you think of?

"Christopher Cross. He sang from the heart, and it was good. But he was kind of treated like a joke within the industry, it felt like. He wrote songs for a lot of people. His first album was fucking great, and he wasn't no show pony—he was famous because his music was great. He was excellent. Big guy. His voice does not match the body. He got stage fright, he got nervous as hell—we know them now as panic attacks. He's a big guy, and he got so pink in the face. He said, 'This happens to me sometimes. I get stage fright.' I said, 'That's cool, now walk with me.' I offered him a shot of liquor, or a toot, or a pill to calm him down, (but) he said no, and I just kept walking him towards the stage. I told Steve Gudis, I said, 'Christopher Cross is having stage fright.' (laughs) And Steve was like, no fucking pills. Steve Gudis and I just talked to Chris Cross, and we got him on stage. Once he was on stage, he was a natural."

When I say that "so-and-so musician had a huge ego," who do you think of?

"Probably Lindsey Buckingham of Fleetwood Mac. He thought really highly of himself. He was a skin-in type of guy, you know what I mean? He didn't care about anything in this world outside his own skin."

Later that evening, from my notes: The Beach Boys are about to come to Greensboro. I was trying to look up corroborating dates for Frank's memories, and I saw in a link that The Beach Boys will pull into town to perform on February 3, 2022, at the Tanger Center in Greensboro. "With more than five decades of touring under their belts, The Beach Boys have performed more concerts than any major rock band in history. The Beach Boys are led by Mike Love, who, along with longtime member Bruce Johnston, musical director Scott Totten, Brian Eichenberger, Christian Love, Tim Bonhomme, John Cowsill, Keith Hubacher and Randy Leago, continue the legacy of the iconic band. This concert will not feature Brian Wilson." In my mind, Brian Wilson gives the Dikembe Mutombo finger wag to the idea of going to sound check and rehearsal.

Regarding Frank's memory, it's elliptical. He comes across as sincere, and he also comes across as an older man who has snorted a lot of cocaine. He is Florida Man. One day, he's saying, "Pink Floyd? Yeah, I worked a show of theirs. I do not remember a single thing about it," and two days later he's telling me an in-depth story about Pink Floyd's lead man, Roger Waters. In comparison, Kathleen's memory is razor-sharp but with large gaps that have seemingly been blasted out of existence. Frank's is continuous, but as a surface, it has been sand-blasted, bleached, and fried.

Day Fourteen

Kathleen

Are you proud of your life?

"I am. I was a little surprised at how ignored I was once I got sick. The friends from the law firm disappeared. Once I had lost my memory and my ability to be in the courtroom, it was like I had lost all value to them, to the world, which was not a good feeling, as you can imagine. But I remember I probably weighed a hundred pounds in high school, max. I was thin, but I was healthy and I ran cross-country for the high school team. I was something of a star on the cross-country team. I wasn't good at track, I wasn't that quick, but when it came to running cross-country, I was good. It was like being free. It was a great feeling, that rush of thinking your legs will never stop moving. I lost that feeling. I felt like I lost all value, all purpose."

Do you still feel that way?

"I am going to walk on the beach, and I am going to swim this Fourth of July. No, I do not."

You defended innocent people that were being run ragged by an uncaring system. Do you see yourself as being in that situation now because of your health issues?

"I have a great feeling of freedom today because I don't have those people around me who say you should do this, you should do that. I got a total sense of freedom from doing anything I don't want to do. I keep up with my close friends and clients, and I just feel great about it. The most important people that weren't executed are still in my life today. I feel at peace with my life, that these few people care, that we talk every day—that matters more than the well-wishes or casual greetings of a thousand old co-workers who wouldn't piss on you if you were on fire."

The following is an excerpt of a July 29, 2002 article from The National Law Journal:

When Kathleen A. Behan was still in law school, she became involved in assisting Columbia Law School Professor James Liebman in his appellate efforts to overturn death penalty convictions. "The work was important and compelling," she says. It was also influential in determining the path her career would take.

"In law school, I was looking for a job as a death penalty lawyer. I couldn't find one," Behan says. But she did get hired by the American Civil Liberties Union, where she began working in early 1989 as staff counsel on the agency's National Security Litigation Project. She spent the next year "mostly brief-writing," then joined Washington, D.C.'s Arnold & Porter as an associate in 1990.

Arnold & Porter had a decades-long reputation of handling major pro bono criminal defense appeals. Its lawyers, for instance, won the 1963 landmark U.S. Supreme Court decision in Gideon v. Wainwright. Behan was not drawn solely by the opportunity to work on pro bono matters, she adds. "I wanted to do some civil litigation." She began working on a wide range of matters, including white-collar crime, antitrust and constitutional law.

Behan was part of the team that won an acquittal for General Electric Co. in a federal antitrust action in late 1994. She represented the American Red Cross in blood supply-related litigation. She represents Major League Baseball as trial counsel in copyright royalty arbitrations. And Behan was one of the attorneys for fugitive financier Marc Rich in his successful — and notorious — campaign to gain a pardon in the waning days of the Clinton administration.

But it is in Behan's commitment to pro bono work that she has made the biggest impact. "As soon as I walked into Arnold & Porter I became involved in the Roger Coleman appeal," she says. Coleman was a Virginia man who had been convicted of killing his sister-in-law and sentenced to death.

Soon after Behan signed on, the two attorneys directing the case left the firm, leaving her in charge. Behan represented Coleman in all phases of his second petition for a writ of habeas corpus and his petition for executive clemency. Coleman was executed in May 1992, but it didn't deter Behan from continuing her involvement in death penalty or other pro bono litigation. About 20 percent of her practice is devoted to pro bono work. She is also co-chairwoman of the Arnold & Porter pro-bono committee and supervises its impact litigation.

Behan represents the American Council of the Blind in its efforts to force the Washington Metropolitan Area Transit Authority to install safety provisions for the blind or visually impaired. She is a lead counsel for the plaintiffs in the litigation against the state of Mississippi seeking to force a modernization of the state's indigent defense system. She is representing a class of mentally ill inmates at the Angola prison in Louisiana alleging violations of their civil rights.

Now a partner, Behan currently represents James Dennis, who was convicted in 1992 in Philadelphia of the murder of a teenage girl in a robbery and sentenced to death. The appeal focuses on the claim that the prosecutor "handpicked jurors based on racial identity and stereotypical reasoning." So far, Behan says, "I have not had any of my inmates come off death row. I certainly hope it will happen with Dennis."

I hope Kathleen lets me keep the reality of her situation in this story. She's in diapers every day. Her life is not easy. She has a nurse, in addition to Frank; she's a lovely woman who visits every morning. The nurse drives a car with Vermont plates—Green Mountains, represent. While I'm there, Frank encourages the nurse to growl. He's like a garrulous drill sergeant around them. He yells that they're growling to frighten away the fear, and they all growl. It's bravery, compassion, perhaps a little flirting, and it was wonderful to witness. That Kathleen needs to wear diapers reflects not at all on who she was, who she is, who she will be. I am privileged to have spent this time with her. She reminds me of my Aunt Bonnie, twice a cancer survivor and the toughest person I've ever met.

Today it's Kathleen who has surprised me, the phone already ringing.

"I'm calling Jimmy Dennis."

Jimmy Dennis: "Kitty?"

Kathleen: "Jimmy, hey."

Jimmy: (emotional) "Kitty, it is so good to hear your voice. I love you with all of my heart. I think about you every day. It's because of you that I'm home with my family."

Kathleen: "Ah, Jimmy, you're making me cry."

— Andrew Mallin —

Jimmy: "Your writer guy there?"

Hello Mr. Dennis, I'm Andrew.

Jimmy: "Hello, Andrew, nice to meet you. Kitty coming into my life was nothing short of a blessing. Before she came, every single attorney I had not only lied to me but they would let me down. Everyone in the city would talk about my innocence. It was like everyone in Philly knew, but everyone is part of the game. You can't defend a guy when you're going out for tea and crumpets with the other side. This was a hot political case, and this was people looking to make their names. My lawyer filed a horrible PCR (post-conviction relief) petition on my behalf."

Kathleen: "It was the worst thing I'd ever seen."

Jimmy: "It was something I could've done myself. My attorney was basically working with the other side. The first time we met face-to-face, Kitty knew. This is the beauty of Kitty's spirit—it's not like I was offering her anything, I had nothing to offer—Kitty knew and she helped. She told me that she not only believed me, she believed in me. Man, I needed that. I was being jumped and attacked in jail, I was getting called uppity and all kinds of things, I lost some of my hearing forever, I got teeth knocked out. Kitty said, 'I believe in you, and there's not going to be a single person on your team who does not believe in you the way you believe in you.' She said, 'You will be respected.' And she did every single thing she said she was going to do. Every. Single. Thing. Andrew, do I have to tell you how rare the person is who does that? The people Kitty had me meet with were all prepared and knew what we were up against. She built this wonderful team of human beings. She lead the charge."

Kathleen: "These kids were three of the best young lawyers Arnold & Porter had. They have gone on to have great careers, but I (have) never seen three kids just out of law school put in work like that. They worked so hard."

Jimmy: "Kitty and these lawyers made nine years of miscarriage of justice disappear. So the judge said to Kitty, 'I'm only giving you three months.' Kitty turned to the judge, and said, 'Okay fine.' Now, that's a lot of pressure. You're talking about a death penalty case that had been on death row for nine years, and she needed to do all the research from scratch, cleaning up the mess of the public defenders from the beginning. When I got the finished product, I was expecting a folder. So the loudspeaker in my death row cell squawks, and they say, 'Your case work is here,' and I was expecting a folder, and these guys are saying, pardon my French, but they're saying, 'We're not bringing you this shit.' So I'm like, what is going on? So I look at this mountain of files. There were boxes. I started crying when I saw it. I called Kitty, and I just said thank you. I was tired of people saying the truth and then acting like they don't know the truth. So the thing with Kitty, she was the first person to say I was innocent on paper. All these other lawyers would try to say some argument or another made sense, even when they agreed with me that I'm innocent. They would go away and put any other words on the documents. Nobody ever stuck behind me like that."

Kathleen is silently crying.

Jimmy: "Judge Anita Brody was the woman who heard the NFL's CTE (chronic traumatic encephalopathy) case. Judge Anita Brody got the case, and we finally got the decision in 2013. The first line of the legal opinion reads as follows, "James A Dennis was wrongfully imprisoned for a crime he did not commit." That was a moment that I had waited for, that my family had waited for. It felt like all my life."

That seemed to be my cue because I was suddenly finding the room to be very dusty.

Kathleen: "I have never seen a ruling like that before or after. The judge will usually spackle over things by talking about a lack of evidence. This was different."

Jimmy: "So what happens next is there was a prosecutor by the name of Seth Williams. He had political aspirations, and he appealed the decision. He ran in Philly and sold himself to black voters about appealing for change and being a leader for change. Yet, here he is in the courtroom trying to railroad me. That was a bad day, that was a low feeling, but Kitty never let me drop my head. The lawyers that Kitty put in place—Kitty had her eye on the talent from the law firm, she put the best of the best together, and they became my family. They brought their kids to visit me. They still talk to me to this day. Our families are friends. I don't think I need to tell you how unusual that is. For us all to have each other's home phone numbers and their kids calling me Uncle Jimmy? That's the product of special people."

Kathleen: "Tell him about the good, bad, and ugly of coming home."

Jimmy: "I came home, but didn't come home the way I should have because of corruption. The guy I talked about went to jail for six months for his corruption—six months for trying to get a man wrongfully imprisoned for life and knowingly doing it. That's justice? I set out to do the things I told Kitty I would do when she asked me what I would do if I was free. When you Google my name you see it says 'R & B artist.' I didn't want to be the guy who was just 'the innocent guilty man.' Nobody in this country is who they wanted to be as a child. What I mean by that is that when you go through something like that, you come out different on the other side. I came out on the other side. I was with my family three years ago, and one of Kitty's old assistants called me, to check in, to see if I was alright, because Kitty had created a family that I was a part of. She is simply brilliant. She is like a sister to me. Kitty understood from the day we spoke that this could not be treated like another case, that because of what we were up against we needed more, and we took up the mantra that we are family. That's what got us through. They respected what I was saying, and so years later a friend called me and she says, 'You know what it says when I Google you?' and I say, 'No,' and she says, 'It says R&B artist.' I wasn't defined by what I had not done in my life. I was no longer defined by crimes I had not committed. I got a little emotional there."

"Since then, I'm proud to say, I've been helping other innocent projects. William Veasy is an innocent man who came home. [Willie Veasy was convicted in Philadelphia in 1993 of second-degree murder and sentenced to life without parole.] His sister came up to me crying, and (saying), 'I just need your help.' I was in some innocence symposium, so I did what Kitty would've done: I started researching. I read everything I could about the case, and I helped to do what I could. William Veezy came home in 2019.

"Seth Williams took a plea deal and served six months at most. The horrible thing is, he's trying to ingratiate himself back into Philly politics. Look at him now. He's back out there, doing his thing. Whenever there's crime going on in the city, the media runs to him and he runs to the media. You can quote me on this—fuck that guy. He does not believe in anyone but himself.

"My dad died while I was on death row. They wouldn't let me out to pay my last respects. My mother had never asked me for anything, and she said, 'Everyone knows you're innocent, and your little girl needs you now.' She urged me to come home however I could, before it was too late. My daughter says, 'I waited for you every day by the door, looking out the window, hoping you would come. Every day. All I want is you to come home and have a relationship with your granddaughter and me.' I don't know if you can imagine the horror of trying to be a father for exactly fifteen minutes a week over the phone. I had a family, and then I was gone for something I didn't do.

"My mother was in hardship at that time. She needed a lot of help. My daughters were struggling with mental health issues, thoughts of suicide; it was a bad time. So I made the agonizing decision to come home by taking a deal. The alternative was to fight for my innocence, while remaining locked away from my family. This is not a deal like any other deal—I never stood up in court and never admitted to any guilt. What happened with me was every single word—and this is a note of public record—every single word that said 'guilty' was redacted from the document. My innocence was read into the record. Then the judge admonished the prosecution, who were in the room. Andrew, I started crying, and the judge kinda paused what she was doing, and she held up the two briefs, and she said, 'You are innocent, and you have nothing to be ashamed of or cry over.' And that was it, and I went home.

"A couple years later, an innocent man came before a judge, Judge Barbara McDermott. This guy was put in the situation that I was, and he was going to be put in the situation where he would plead guilty to something he did not do to avoid jail. The judge took the sentence away from the D.A., and she set that man, Terrance Lewis, free, and days later Terrance Lewis called me. The judge had said it was because of the precedent

Kitty set in her defense of me that he was going free. That's all because of Kitty."

Kathleen: "Do you remember—I said I know you're going to be a musician when you get out—but do you remember what I told you your future could be?"

Jimmy: (laughs) "You told me to be a lawyer. She offered me a job as a paralegal. I appreciated that, just . . . (sounds of crying) . . . I'm so grateful for everything that you've done for my life. My life—I'm suffering now, my family doesn't have everything they need—but I'm here, I'm talking to all of you, and I'm blessed. I'm here with my fiancée, I'm here for my daughters, and I'm here for my mother. That's what matters."

Kathleen: "Send them all my love and best wishes for happiness."

Jimmy: (clearing his throat) "I'm gonna do that, and you're gonna keep getting better, alright? I can't tell you how good it is to hear your voice again".

Kathleen: (trying real hard not to cry) "Jimmy, you take care."

Jimmy: "You too, Kitty. Hey Andrew, you're writing a book about someone who changed the legal game. She set precedents that are in place today going forward, but what's most rare about Kitty Behan is she sees another person as a person. Most people see others in terms of what they can do for you. Kitty saved my life by seeing me as I am, and you quote me on that."

Once we've composed ourselves, I stand to walk Kathleen from the interview room. She pats my shoulder as I wipe my face dry. She says she wants to give me one thing to take, and we walk toward the sun porch, late morning sunlight toasting this nook sheltered from the wind. I'm half expecting her to hand me her father's book on life. We've all three discussed photographing her father's book. We all want that book to make it into this book. Instead, it is a small black book that Kathleen hands me. It is the Alcoholics Anonymous book; the story of how many thousands of men and women have recovered from alcoholism. Third edition. AA World Services, Inc. New York City. 1976.

Handwritten above this in bold block letters are the words "You Are Not Alone Anymore."

The only other handwritten note is a section of page 139, which has been bracketed, "To me, this incident illustrates lack of understanding as to what really ails the alcoholic, and lack of knowledge as to what part employers might profitably take in salvaging their sick employees."

I thank her and tell her I will keep it safe, that I will return it with this manuscript. She nods, lightly punches me in the shoulder, and heads for the sunny spot out of the wind on the deck—her place.

I make my excuses and need five minutes to compose myself. Then I'm ready to see Frank for the last time.

*****

Frank

Were you upset about the peanut butter cup because Kathleen might have had a seizure?

"No, it's because she lied about it. It's something in me that I don't like the liars. It started young in me. There are so many con artists and liars that I saw from an early age. I learned to read them, and I learned to dislike the con artists and liars. It's like going to a restaurant that uses the real ingredients, and one that says it's serving steak and really it's serving ground chuck. The second restaurant isn't going to get the repeat business.

"The shipyard, normally you get paid every two weeks, so every two weeks in the drug business you need to be ready. There are big buildings there in the ship yard. Usually, I just liked to give a pound of weed to a guy. I didn't like working in smaller amounts than pounds. A smart guy can sell a pound just within the shop they're in. This was more of a peaceful business, marijuana and hashish. It was a peaceful business and a great business. I would pay the guys at the gates to the Norfolk gates—they're not military, they're shipyard police officers. George Washington Tavern was about a half mile from the back gate. The cop who worked the back gate was one hell of an alcoholic. We would drop off his money at the tavern whenever we needed to meet up with him. One time, we stole a couple pallets of copper from the shipyard, and the guy at the back gate waved us out, and as he did, he said, 'I gotta see you tonight.' And he's pretending to look at what's on our truck, and he noticed the forklift. See, we lifted these two pallets up, and then the forklift, we couldn't really figure out, so we took it out. This was Mike Agnar and I with this big flatbed truck an uncle lent me for the occasion.

"Working in the shipyard is anonymous. People didn't pay any attention to you because you had a hard hat, badge. There are a couple hundred contractors like that in the shipyard every day, so you could get away with anything. Nobody is looking at you.

"I can tell you a lot of stories about Prince because I was around him a lot. I was with him in San Francisco, California, and Prince was almost too famous at this point. He was on the cover of every fucking magazine. I'm wearing suits on this tour. I bought them on the Miracle Mile in Miami.

— Andrew Mallin —

I'm riding shotgun, Jay Bell, Bill Snouffer, and Prince are in the back. I'm shotgun, and we're gonna go into this big hotel in California, so we put a raincoat over Prince so none of the screaming people can take pictures of him. It's that big hotel with all the flags in San Francisco; it's real famous. So Prince tried to go in through this revolving door, and the raincoat got caught in the door, and Prince is making all these "When Doves Cry" sounds, trying to cover himself like Marilyn Monroe over that grate. After that piece of performance art, we take him up to the room. First thing we do is check the suites to see if anyone is in there. At least twice we've found people hiding under the bed on this tour—people were desperate to get near Prince at that point. We did that whole tour with him.

"Every time after a show, Prince would go and watch a video of the show he just did. He would watch the show with a notepad and pen out, and he would make a note about anything that didn't work. He didn't do cocaine, but the whole rest of that group did.

"I like martial arts, so I was real excited when I met Chuck Norris. He was a martial arts guy. I met him on the Prince tour. We went to The Zoo Club in Miami. Me, Bill, and Jay Bell and some Cuban guys were hanging out with Chuck Norris. Chuck Norris wanted to be introduced to Prince, and I said to him, 'Look, Prince is fucked-up.' But Chuck Norris was like, 'It's cool, no big deal. I just want to say hi, and it's no big deal.' Well, Chuck Norris walked over and extended his hand, and Prince, who was sitting down, just looked at the hand, then looked away. I got pretty close to popping Prince a couple times, and that was one of them. Like, 'Look man, he's trying to shake your hand, just shake his fucking hand.' Well, Prince was in a right mood that night. See, one of the Cuban guys who was there with Gilbert was dancing up a storm with Sheila E, and Prince did

— Rockstars and Executions —

not like that one bit. So the party is (in) full fucking swing, there are women and famous people and everyone there, and a confused Chuck Norris is just trying to introduce himself, and Prince stands up and starts saying, soft as can be, 'I would like the club to myself now.' Well, Bill Snouffer called me over, and we're listening to Prince, and he just keeps saying, soft and softer, 'I would like to have the club to myself now.' So, um, okay. I find Gilbert and I tell him, 'Look, Prince is a big softie; he's upset about this here party; let's all go to some other club.' Well, Gilbert's friend was like, 'Sure,' and he was gonna take Sheila E with him! So people are starting to leave. Prince had killed the party pretty dead—the music stopped, everyone was a bit confused, but we were gonna go to another club. Gilbert and me and Bill Snouffer agreed he was going to take care of Prince. But then Prince saw Sheila E start to leave, and he started screaming. Like, 'Nooooo, nooooooo.' He's crying. He cried. He was a fucking mess. So I told Gilbert and them I'd see them later. I grabbed Sheila E, and I grabbed the rest of Prince's crew, and Bill Snouffer had Prince, and he was carrying him like a baby. Prince was having a full-on fucking tantrum, and I'll just never ever forget the look on Chuck Norris' face as Bill Snouffer carried a crying Prince past him. Chuck Norris was good at martial arts, you know that?

"Fleetwood Mac all liked cocaine, for sure. I was in Tennessee with them. I had met them in Virginia, done security, and sold them a bunch of coke. Then I was with Stevie Nicks and the whole group. She was cool and everything. Maybe we did fifteen to twenty shows with them. I would give them their packages, and something happened where she was in the limo. I think what it was is Stevie had run out of coke before the show, or maybe it was just after a show, because you can't really sing on cocaine—you can't get the vocals right, you can't get in sync. Before, because I would walk them off stage, Stevie Nicks told me to get with her later. Sometimes you give them the drugs when you hand them a towel as they come off the stage. So I knocked on the limo, and Stevie and another woman were going at it pretty good. The limo is still at the venue. We're in the basement of the venue in the parking lot, so it's quiet. I just whistled a tune and walked off, and I waited for them to finish.

"One night, I was with Fleetwood Mac in West Virginia. They were in the bar, and there was a lot of fucking and backstabbing going on with that band—everyone knows how fucked up it was with all them. Anyway, they're going to their limos, and again, it's a band where there's not one limo with two band members in it. Everyone had to have their own limo; they couldn't stand to be around each other —that bad."

Frank calls Jay Bell.

Frank: "Jay Bell did the *Purple Rain* tour."

Jay Bell: "I was off work in Queens, and these two beautiful women walk by—they didn't give me the time of day. I'm being friendly, and they're like, 'We don't give a shit.' Well, just then the purple bus came and picked me up; it's Bill Snouffer, and it's time to work. Now those two women were screaming to get on the bus!"

Frank: "Tell the writer man about Prince and women."

Jay: "A lot of people lost their job trying to fuck with Sheila E. Prince was not having it. (laughs) A lot of people liked Sheila E. Craziest thing on the *Purple Rain* tour, Jerome was on the tour with us. That was one of the biggest tours in America, yet we couldn't stay in Birmingham, Alabama, 'cause most of the fans were white ladies, so Prince was getting lots of death threats. Well, we talked it out, and we said, 'Fuck it,' because Prince didn't want to back down. So we played the show in Birmingham,

— Rockstars and Executions —

Alabama, but then we stayed in Tennessee after the show. That was a dicey show. Look, I'll say this about Prince: he worked my Black ass to death!"

Frank: "You were fearless man, fucking with Prince's women. Take care, Jay."

After he hangs up, I ask Frank about whether he knew Steve Gudis well.

Frank: "I liked Steve very much. I've stayed with him, we went to the Kentucky Derby together. Steve would do a line of coke and clean his apartment. Steve talked like Wolfman Jack a little bit. It was a growl, which is funny cause Steve is a short, kinda chubby Jewish guy—not chubby, but you know. Anyway, he was a funny sight after doing a line of coke, running around cleaning things in his skivvies.

"Steve Gudis was a professional. He and I did some stuff, but he was very, very good at what he did. My first experience with Jethro Tull was one of the first concerts I ever worked in the business that felt modern. They were the first band to do this: they had two units. I think KISS was the second band to do it. So they would have a full set of riggers, electricians, managers, and while they were doing that, their second production team would be in the next venue already getting it ready for the second night of shows. So they were putting on a big show every night. Guys like Steve changed things.

"I forgot to ask him about it, but John Campbell worked for a guy named Chip Monk. Chip had cut his bones putting together Woodstock. Chip was the production manager guy for Pink Floyd and the Stones for a long time.

"You wanted to know what Tennessee was like? Country music acts are more rock and roll than the rock and roll acts. The country music guys took it to another fucking level. But then, I don't know, the rock and roll guys had some issues too.

"Rick James is not about fighting at all. He was about women and drugs. So when you ask me who was an asshole in the music business, Rick James would not say boo to a butterfly if he thought the butterfly would hit back. I think for me the British crew was that little bit wilder. Guys like Mick and all them, they really didn't give too much of a fuck about the women, which I understand sounds ridiculous, but bear with me. They were much more interested in the drugs. With Mick, I had three women that I had to transport, so it's not like he was going celibate or turning into a monk. There were three women Mick was with on that tour, and according to the girls, Mick would mostly just talk all night. At one point, he got into heroin. So yeah, he was talking all night long about God knows what."

Where did you encounter the highest percentage of bad people: the drug business, the auto business, or the rock and roll business?

"The answer has to be all three. There are good people in every walk of life, and there are con artists and thieves in any industry.

"Sorry, I was talking about the Kentucky Derby with Steve Gudis. We meet, I fly in, and I actually have the coke on me in the jewelers vest, which I normally didn't do."

Fly with cocaine?

"Yeah. Normally I tried to avoid it like the plague, but I wanted to go to the Derby, and Steve invited me last minute. I had a pound on me in sixteen little bags, the highest-end shit. You ever see *Bad Lieutenant* with Harvey Keitel? There was the R-rated and X-rated versions. Well, this stuff was the X-rated.

"At the airport, I got picked up by a limo, and there's a nice-looking woman driving it. So this lady driver is in a full uniform. I was pretty keyed up, and I liked that a lot. I said, does she drive normally? She said no, it's her husband's company and she's only been driving because it's the Derby. She had been driving all day yesterday, then last night, and she's so tired she can't keep her eyes open. So I said, 'I might have something that can help with that.'

"Have you ever heard of a coke bullet? It's just like a little tube, like a bullet casing, and you snort it right up. Well, she said that sounds good, so she did a bump, then she did a couple bumps more, all while she was driving. I climbed into the front seat, and we did a spin around, then we ended up at this lady's house. I called Steve, and so Steve and this other girl met us there. The Kentucky Derby is a huge deal, so there were a lot of stuff going on the week before the Derby. So Steve had a couple small shows going on, but he had time to party too. Steve is waiting to meet me, and the limousine driver had a girlfriend of hers meet us at her house.

"So it got a little wild there, things got a little freaky. I was looking at both women, and I said, 'Y'all look really hot, can I see some more?' Steve is a short Jewish guy, funny as hell. He's got this raspy dark voice. He's some guy. I had given Steve most of the ounces out of my vest at this point, and he was pretty excited, so I took the woman who had driven me. We went into her bedroom, and we're having a little fun. What did I care that she was married? I broke an ounce of coke into a little bowl like you'd eat cereal out of, and we were in her bedroom, and occasionally she'd go sliding off the bed, and she'd just dip her fingers in the bowl and then come back to bed. Steve's getting wild in the next room. His girl was running in and out of the rooms. And the girl I'm with gets on the coke bad. She's done too much. And then the front door opens, and there's a guy there and he is pissed. He's saying, 'That's my wife, motherfucker.' I said, 'I didn't know. I respect you. I don't know you, but I understand what's going on here now.' So I said, 'You do what you gotta do if you want to hit me, but I'll hit you right back since I didn't know you.' So he was pissed, but he kinda let it slide. I grabbed Steve's clothes off the floor, and we got out of there. The guy didn't want to get goofy because Steve is a big promoter, a very big promoter, and this guy owned a limo company.

"So we ended up in a VIP box at the Kentucky Derby, and Steve and I, well, we might have let the coke go to our heads a little bit. I mean, that was the time to have fun, but well, we get up there, and we look around, and everyone is dressed up real nice. Steve and I were dressed like cowboys. I don't really remember where we went or how we got the duds, but we had these full fucking cowboy outfits: boots with spurs, everything. The mint juleps kinda calm you down and smooth you out a little bit.

"I'm kinda looking around, and a guy sticks his arm out of nowhere and stops me. I nearly broke the guy's arm for putting his hands on me, you know? He'd basically slammed me in the chest. I had the cowboy hat on; this thing was fucking huge, and I couldn't hardly see from under it. Well, this guy had hit me in the chest to stop me, and I don't think, I just tried to snap his arm off. So Steve fucking screamed my name. He yelled, 'Hammer!' So I look up, and Gerald Ford is about two arms-lengths away. The guy who had stopped me was one of them secret service! Steve came up and was real pleasant and made some excuses, and we got out of that VIP box pretty quick. Steve Gudis was a funny guy, like I said, and he almost had those secret service guys crack a smile. Would've been the first fucking time in their lives. Well, Gerald Ford didn't seem too impressed with me or my outfit or just my general behavior (laughs), but we had a lot of fun that day. I remember Steve and I laughing until we nearly fell over once we'd got back to our VIP box."

Make any bets on the Derby?

"Yeah, I won the Platinum Silver bet—that was the name of the horse. I remember we were high as shit, and I bet on Platinum Silver because I was in the jewelry business and it seemed like a good fit."

What did you do with the winnings?

"Just blow it like usual. Actually, what was that horses name? Oh shit, I got it. Silver Charm was his name. It was the 1997 Kentucky Derby."

What did blowing money look like for you?

"Well, for me, that means I'd go out and buy a couple cars. You have got to get this concept into your head: I made almost a hundred grand on every kilo, and back then, the stuff was so good we could cut it with the machete and we would double it, every time. So half of everything I sell is shit I've basically got for free, and now you're turning that into a hundred grand. So you get used to doing twenty, thirty kilos a month; that's a lot of fucking money. Back then, a Ferrari was only like, forty thousand dollars in Europe, a Porsche about the same. I had a million dollars in cash under the patio of my parent's house. That was my emergency stash for buying shit. I had a bunch of stashes of cash at family member's houses. That was the emergency bad weather money. But the million bucks under the patio was for emergency purchases, either for the business or just because. Because when you're making that much money every month, you sometimes get a hair across your ass to buy something new.

"Things started small, then they got big. Going way back, there came a time when I was having a hard time getting bulk amounts of weed in Virginia. I had this guy in Boston, but it was a bad time. See, they were spraying this Paraquat shit on all the fields, so there was a real shortage. So I drove down from Portsmouth, Virginia, to Tucson, Arizona. It was me in my car and two guys of mine with other cars of mine. We drove the whole fucking way. I put a CB radio in each of my Cadillacs. And it was scary. I was still young then, and we had these three Cadillacs that had everything customized. We even took the wires out behind the back seats of the Cadillacs because we wanted to load every fucking inch of these things. I had customized them to hell and back: new shocks and everything because I wanted them to ride as easy as they could with a couple hundred pounds of weed in each of 'em. So we met these guys in Tuscon, and I knew there and then I would not do another deal with them ever again. Something happened there that I can't get into—a couple people had to get hurt there and it wasn't me. So driving back, the three of us were shaky. We were worried about the cars breaking down from all the weight, and we were worried about the fuckers we'd just left behind making trouble for us. Scumbags call the cops.

"So we get a couple hundred miles into the trip back to Virginia, and one of my drivers starts cracking up. He got so nervous he couldn't drive. He got the shakes bad. We were distancing ourselves a little bit, a few miles, so there wasn't just three identical Cadillacs in a weird-looking convoy. So I had given my drivers a little bit of cash and told them to meet me at some restaurants we knew on the Tennessee state border; they would be a good place to meet up. The guy who cracked up was an Irish guy who was from Portsmouth. So I got the Irish guy on a plane, got him the fuck out of there. He was stressing and saying the cops are going to get us and all this. Now, before I put him on the plane, I said. 'You know we're supposed to be brothers? You wouldn't flip me? Because if you do, it's you and it's your family.' I let him know that any thoughts about flipping on me or my cars would be a bomb going off. I told him to relax and enjoy the fucking flight. So we drop him off at this little airport, I don't even remember where this was, but it wasn't a big city. Anyway, we drop him off, and I put the car he was driving in a storage unit for three months—with everything in it.

"That drive was bad from beginning to end. It was scary, and there was a lot of risk in it. It was not good business.

"Uncle Nikolai? I got introduced to him through Gilbert Hernandez. Gilbert was my first foray into the cocaine business. So Gilbert invites me to this huge fucking party at Uncle Nikolai's house, this huge outdoor party. It was for a little kid's birthday or some religious something. So I'm there and meeting a lot of people who are calling me '*gringo*,' you get me? And two guys are at the party, and they fall out. So this party is huge, and you can hear the guns go off. I was thinking it was the cops because a lot of screaming and hollering started while I was just looking around the horse pen. When the shooting started, I was asking the guys around me what the fuck was going on and none of them speak English. Well, eventually I found Gilbert. Turns out two guys who had a beef had been drinking and maybe sniffing something, and they decided to settle their beef. Uncle Nikolai was fucking pissed.

"So soon after that, we started with the car carriers. We would have junk cars or whatever—the cars didn't matter, but we made some money on them too—but we would ship the cars on the car carrier trucks and in each car would be a bunch of kilos. So we kinda became a little group. Uncle Nikolai was happy with me because I was moving so much weed and coke from them to Virginia. After a while, Nikolai asked me, kinda as a favor and I was too stupid to say no or to be afraid; but he asked me . . . but kinda told me that I was going to be a 'wrastler' for him. You see, this is not a cowboy job. We're not talking about cows. You go out, and you get people, and you bring them back to where they tell you to take them, then they would question the guy or woman or whatever. Sometimes you'd drive them back to where you stashed them, sometimes you wouldn't.

"Uncle Nikolai was an older guy, maybe in his 70s, very rough-looking. Rough-cut but solid guy. He looked windburnt, you know? He barely spoke English. He always carried, like, a snuff box of coke. So that's fine around us, but this fucking guy would be in, like, a Florida grocery store, and he would take out that snuff box of coke without even looking around, and he would just take a snort right there. He was fucking nuts. I never knew what country Nikolai was from—he would sometimes say he was Colombian, but I'm pretty fucking sure he was Cuban. Lots of Cubans are cowboys, you know? I don't like horses, but lots of Cubans liked horses and were actual cowboys. Uncle Nikolai had a stable; horses, he fucking loved them.

"The Cubans ran DHL in Miami. Packages, and I mean big packages, would just go through DHL clean as you please. There were like two sniffing dogs in all of Miami back then."

Ever participate in an orgy?

"Yea, a few of them. They weren't really my thing. I like, you know, to get to know somebody.

Tell me about the Playboy Club Miami.

"Fuck orgies, that place was better—the best. I made a lot of good connections at that club. There was more to it than just women. Gilbert was a GQ-looking guy and he loved women, but his brother Pete was just about being a gangster. So when Gilbert and I would go there and anytime I took someone like Steve Gudis there, it was the fucking best. We had so much coke there, not in plain sight but there was plenty if you wanted it.. I mean that was a fucking wild place. Studio 54 had some sister club in Miami. The original was in New York, but they had some other club in Miami. Between that club and the playboy club, all my guys had a lot of fun.

"You had to be a member to get in there at the Playboy Club, but I got a bunch more people in. Bebito had the Cuban restaurant on Flagler. They had all the phones on the table, so we would all sit in the back and just watch people come and go. Then when we wanted to kick it up a notch, we'd go over to the Playboy Club. And I would bring all of my guys over there, and some of my guys were not from the Miami scene, you know? I had some regular middle-class cocaine dealers in my ranks, and these guys could each make a million dollars a year, and so when we went to the Playboy Club, you should've seen them, these country boys. Phew. The guys who are still alive still talk about that club."

How old were you the first time you got high?

"With Mike Agnar's brother, probably when I was nineteen. I trained all the time. I wasn't a doper, but I smoked a joint with Jerry Agnar. Jerry had just come back from Vietnam. We were with his friend Carl. Carl had just come back from Vietnam. These guys had been drafted when they were eighteen, so they were still kids. It's crazy to think about how much the Vietnam War boosted the drug industry in this country. See, Jerry and Carl had gone, and when they were in-country they had smoked a shit-load of weed, so when they got back? They wanted weed.

"I don't think people understand how tightly tied the weed and coke trade in America is to the Vietnam War, and I'm not talking about users, about guys who want to get high. A bunch of guys came home with no fear—or so full of fear they didn't give a fuck about anything, you know? What's the threat of a bid in jail when you've spent night after night wondering if it's you who's gonna get sniped on patrol, if it's you who's going to step on something and blow the fuck up? What's a couple years or a couple cops with guns against that? Then you add the money you can make, the power that money gives you. I mean, hey, look at January sixth—there were a bunch of people there who had gone to war and they've come back, and what do they have to lose? So when a man stands on stage and says it's all somebody's fault, first of all they're going to listen, and they're gonna think they got nothing to lose tearing it down on his say-so. And hey, (laughs) if you've got money in your pocket, or people think they can make a lot of money off you, people will listen to you. No matter how stupid the shit you're saying is, people will listen. (laughs) My guys must've listened to me a couple goofy nights after a couple sniffs too many or whatever, and man, they must have just been wondering what in the fuck I was talking about. (laughs) But they listen, they show respect, because I've got cash and I've got the means to make more cash tomorrow. People will follow me if I'm showing them that cash, no matter how off my tits or my rocker I am. They can even know I'm off my rocker, wouldn't matter if you got that wad of cash and the promise of more."

If you had a time machine, would you change anything about your life?

"Yeah. I should've never did any cocaine, ehh, because it's, you know, too dangerous of a drug—let's say that. Cocaine put me into situations where I almost killed a couple more people. It re-wired my mind. We used to say it was like having wires in your brain, and the coke burns the rubber insulation off your wires, so the wires start misfiring. It takes your body to the extreme. Like, we're just talking about the Kentucky Derby? I didn't sleep for three days there. Three days and three nights, no sleep, so when I got back to Virginia, I had to go to a doctor. He gave me some downers, nearly killed me."

Did you ever work out on cocaine?

"One fucking time."

You seem upset about it.

"I remember it completely. Oh yeah, it was a big no-no. My parents lived in Bowers Hill in Virginia, and in the garage I had two heavy bags and a couple speed bags and a couple jump ropes, and some of my cousins and all of the kids in the neighborhood would come over to work out, and I had these fuckers rolling. So one day I'm feeling a little tired. This is real goofy. There was a tree on the side of the road that had a crevice in it, and that's where I would stick an ounce or two of cocaine for the guys. I would just say, 'Go to the tree.' So one day I went to the tree and did a couple lines, and I took off on a run on a sprint. I sprinted like the last three miles. I could not slow down. I thought I was going to have a fucking heart attack. Trying to calm down—it was that good of the cocaine—I eventually ran into the marsh. There's canals back there. I fucking ran into that shit and was splashing that dismal swamp water on my face because, holy shit, I was revved up. That was the last time I ever worked out on coke. That was real early on too. No, coke was just to celebrate like a good job that was done or with the rock and roll guys."

Did you ever get fat, coke skinny, or otherwise out of shape?

"No. I might have put on a few extra pounds. I got out of control a few times, but I don't know, I think I was always muscular. Working out for a few hours every day balances me.

"So one day I go to this tattoo artist in Greensboro, and there's this famous artist called Little John—famous tattoo artist—and he was in the Hell's Angels. He talked to me about training with him and his guy Mike. I called him Mike Angel. He was younger and earning his buttons or whatever the hell the Angels call it—you know, his initiation. So it was Little John, Mike Angel, and this guy they called Tick Tock. Tick Tock was a kinda scary guy. He got the name from having a short fuse. But he was fine with me; they all three were fine with me. They were big guys, but they were interested in the martial arts and moving up in powerlifting. So I had these three Hell's Angels training with me. We got tight. They went with a code of ethics, they would take care of business. But get this: never, ever, did we talk drug trade between us. But it was available, it just didn't happen. We were focused on the training. Mike was like me, in his heart he was scared of the drugs."

Scared?

"We'd rather be working out than getting fucked-up or fucking someone up. Tick Tock was doing a fair amount of cocaine. Little John had a big place on the outer edge of Greensboro. He had a wife who was beautiful, all tattooed-up. She had a little liking for me, and Little John put the brakes on that real quick. So one day Little John came in, and he was not right. He looked at me with these death eyes, and he goes to me, 'Frank, I need some help.' What can I do? He said, 'Well, I'm back on the fucking drugs,' and he said, 'I might not be here much longer.' He was on heroin that day. So it was only later I found out what had happened, what had went bad. What happened was it was a no-no to mess with another Hell's Angels wife; it's a death sentence for the guy. So a little after he made some mistake with some guy's wife, he's staying up all nights, he's got these huge floodlights on at his house all night, he's telling me he's sleeping with a shotgun and his pistol. He started doing heroin and cocaine at the same time. He was spinning the fuck out, but still coming to our early morning lifting sessions. So I was at the gym late in the afternoon one day with Little John's wife, and I went to the bathroom, and then I came back to keep training with her. Well, when I came back, Little John's pretty tattooed wife was completely naked. I told her, 'I really want to, but this is not a good time.' So a little while after that, I stopped training her. I kept training Mike and Tick Tock, and a little while later I asked where Little John was, and they told me there was a little problem there. So there was this woman who worked at the bank next door, and a couple days or weeks after I stopped training her, she—Little John's wife—slipped the bank teller a note, asking me to talk to her since she was scared as fuck. So then a guy in Hell's Angels showed up to her house—I heard it later from her and Tick Tock in pieces. Well, the guy in Hell's Angels went to Little John. Little John's method of death was suicide. It wasn't exactly, though, you see, because this guy from the Hell's Angels goes to see Little John about his mortal sin, and it was his gun he gave Little John. You know? 'Do it yourself or I'll do it.' Because Little John had slept with the wife of another biker. So I never saw Little John again. A couple weeks after that, his wife got in touch with me, and well, we started getting together.

"So a couple weeks after that, a guy I don't know comes to my yoga studio in Greensboro, and he said, 'You're gonna steer clear of that goofy bitch.' I looked at him, and well, I thought about pulling my pistol because this guy is threatening me in my place, (but) I mean, shit, I had a flock of women. What the fuck do I need with trouble from the Hell's Angels? Beth was her name. So I looked at the guy and I kinda smiled, and I said, 'Maybe you're right.' This was right around the time the Angels started moving a lot of crystal meth. They just were not worth fucking with, no matter how fine Beth was. So I talked to Tick Tock and Mike Angel, and they were tight with me still, but they understood. That was the end of training with them."

Did you buy your first gun?

"What, you think my dad gave me one for Christmas? Yes. I bought all my guns. Nobody ever gave me a pistol. Once I became a felon, it just became a different place where I would buy my guns. (laughs) You see, once you're a felon, it's mighty hard to buy a gun, but that's no problem. It's who you know. Guns that don't exist are all around us. I never had a gun license. I never had anything like that. (laughs) I carried a .45 every day of my adult life."

You think it's safe to talk about people like Uncle Nikolai and Mama?

"Yes, because they're dead. What do I have to lose?"

I mean, look at me. I don't have much of anything to lose either, but I still feel like I want to hide under the table rather than talk about those people, especially on paper.

"Put some fire in your belly before you're gone. They're dead. And it's like the bull—you know, Gotti—or that Boston guy (Whitey Bulger). He didn't last but two days in prison. Check that out: the Boston mob hated that fucker because he was a rat-type guy, I don't think he lasted two days in prison. Well, he was pretty old too. This is mostly the '80s or later we're talking about, you and I. It's history. Gotti was talking about all that shit. It's already out there. That people brought a lot of cocaine and other drugs into the United States, that some people got rich and some people got fucked, is not news."

I noticed you have some books on tantra. Any reading you'd recommend to the kids out there having lame sex? I'm fishing for myself, of course. I stop just shy of trying some flavor of "So I've got this friend, right, and he's wondering . . ."

" Well, I could give them something on that. It's not just about fucking. Tantra is really about expanding and exploring, body and mind. You can explore with a woman, and in high yoga, the tantris, the female, was a higher teacher than the male. In other words, the male and female, the woman, had many different things she would do with her eyes, her body, her different postures. The female principle, or 'shakti,' the female energy, is to explore. Picture being a chef and only knowing how to prepare one entree; being able to cook more dishes would enhance your life. Tantra is no different. It's about enhancing your life, exploring your life."

That was not as helpful as I was hoping for.

"Yes, it was. You just weren't listening. It's about using your senses. Slow down and turn on your senses. Start on the path to great sex by listening to your partner."

What are your three favorite films?

"I wouldn't recommend it to anyone, but *Bad Lieutenant* with Harvey Keitel. If you want to know about drugs and the drug life, that's the movie for you. That movie got being a gangster right. The worst one was the one that Al Pacino was in."

Godfather?

"No! No, that one everyone loved."

Scarface?

— Andrew Mallin —

"That's the one. That was junk. What a stupid fucking movie, and now you've got whole generations who think it's the real fucking deal. I think the movie *Bad Lieutenant* with Harvey Keitel is the closest film has ever come to capturing what it's like to be a gangster. There's an R-rated version and an X-rated version. Both of 'em get it as close to right as I've ever seen."

Did you ever think you were addicted to booze?

"Never. Never. That was the only thing I never really worried about. I never drank hard liquor. When I got into a rich state of mind, shall we say, and was being rich, well, then I was drinking thousand-dollar bottles of wine and stuff like that. But no, I never got addicted to the booze."

Did you ever think you were addicted to drugs?

"I had a problem with drugs for a very long time, let's say that."

Did you ever think you were addicted to sex?

"Never. Actually, it's sorta like when you have a lot of women around you. What I was, uh, because I was near the rock and roll business, I could have had twenty women a night. I can just tell you Billy Joel's first wife wanted to fuck me. I mean, all kinds of shit went down. And then one day, I looked myself in the mirror, and I said, 'Stop conning these women.' If I'm lying to somebody, I'm lying to myself, does that make sense? So I didn't like that after a while. I do like women. I know what a beautiful woman looks like. I don't like a drunk woman at all, or a coked-up woman, not at all. Tammy is like this (moves a hand through the air, level and smooth). That's why I always respected her. Yeah."

Did you ever think you were addicted to power, whether physical or social?

— Rockstars and Executions —

"When I saw someone doing me wrong, let's say, the angry part of me would come out. Liars or people trying to buck up under me for whatever reason, the anger would come out. To say nothing of trying to rob me or kill me. Stuff like that bothers me, and well, you know, that anger just doesn't disappear. I remember a couple years after my brother died in a motorcycle crash with a guy in a car, and I looked for the driver of that car for a couple years. I think that's the closest I got to being addicted to it because I wanted to hurt him, but I also wanted to talk to him first. I was itching to talk to him. I needed to talk to him. And the reality is, what the fuck is he gonna tell me? I wanted my kid brother back. I didn't want to talk to that piece of shit."

How old was your brother when he died in a motorcycle crash?

"Thirteen. He was on the back of a truck driver's Allstate motorcycle—these things were sold by Sears Roebuck. This was sunset on a thirty-five-mile-an-hour road about fifty feet from my parents' house. My parents very, very seldom left the area, but they were in Nags Head, North Carolina. They weren't there, so I was the one in the emergency room with my brother when he died. The driver of the motorcycle was scraped to hell. This motherfucker was a man. He was nearly dead, and he was doing everything he could to try and save my brother—half of his back was gone, he was bleeding everywhere, he'd been fucking dragged by the drunks, but he did everything he could."

Were the two drunk drivers ever arrested?

"I don't think so. I remember my father was out to kill them, and then something stopped him; he just kinda gave up. My father had brothers too, and they wanted to do it. They all wanted to kill those two fuckers. And my father said no. I remember that. Those were some weird days, but my father just put it in the ground with my brother. Maybe my father was a smarter man than I knew then."

Are you medically insured today?

"I have the best insurance."

Are you rich?

"No. I spent a lot of fucking money."

The look on his face is priceless. He's both pissed and proud and stupefied by the memory sensory overload.

"If you had seen some of the things I spent money on . . . "

Are you ever tempted to deal drugs again?

"Here's the thing: I am tempted all the time, but I am not going to do it. If I was going to sell drugs, it would not be cocaine, it would not be heroin, it would not be any pills. If I had wanted to sell high-grade marijuana, that's what I would do. But look around—it's almost legal everywhere around here. Nah, I'm not a cocaine dealer or whatever anymore. I don't like it. It's a simple thing, it's overused, but it's true: there's too much bad karma there. I'm really lucky I didn't go to jail for a lot of reasons, but one thing I should've been in jail for was the people who just did the cocaine and the pills and the heroin. You get sick off that shit, and you still do it because you're wrapped in that warm blanket that says, 'Yeah, this is good.' I regret a lot."

Would you say you are at peace?

"Yeah, I'm mostly at peace. . . . When I'm at my highest peace and having my best thoughts, I'm in the gym. Like the last couple weeks—I know I'd see you each day, so I'd send my thoughts to all these places around the world where I was living or hiding, of all those years where I was tough as fuck and really scared. I was a moving target, and I was loud, and I was stupid as much as I was smart. A lot of the time, the stupid was directly tied to not listening to what I knew within, you know? I mean, being stupid is one thing, being crazy is another. But that thing where you don't do what you know is right? Well, that's the shit that is true stupid. That's the stuff you regret when you look back."

What makes you happy?

"Being alive. And not being in pain. You know they only gave me eight months, and that was over a year ago? I like being alive. You see me walking around all throughout the day. Look, it was easy for me to be a gangster, but to be this type of guy, I was more this type of guy all along. Instead of buying a Ferrari or a Porsche or whatever kind of car or whatever other shit, I am instead working on this car right here (taps on his chest). Tammy knows but very few people know this, I would like to adopt a kid that don't have anything. I want to try and help someone. I can't help with cash or cars or private jets, but I can help. Yesterday, Kitty walked all the way down the block and back and up the stairs and back down the stairs and back up 'em. You believe that? That's impressive shit, man. When I'm training somebody, I'm actually thinking about myself. It's giving me more gifts, does that make sense? I like training people because I can short-word them, just give them little instructions, little techniques, and I can see the results. Seek your highest thoughts always. I like to use the word 'recreate' because I try to recreate myself."

Frank calls Tammy this time.

Frank: "Did you know I was in the drug business when I first met you?"

Tammy: "Kind of, but not really. People would just hint at it because you had all those cars. I think everybody knew."

Frank: "Tammy's uncle told Tammy's mother, 'You know your daughter is dating one of the biggest drug dealers in Virginia?' He did not like me."

Tammy: "My mom didn't need my uncle to say anything. Mom noticed I was driving Mercedes and Porsches, and she was like, 'Where the heck are these cars coming from?'"

Frank: "Did you not like that I was in the drug business?"

Tammy: "I guess I never really minded that much. Although I remember at your condo in Chic's Beach you would tape closed all the cabinets because otherwise you'd spend hours opening and closing them, opening and closing them, swearing you were looking for something. Everyone knew he was in a different frame of mind then."

Frank hangs up, and then his brain makes one of those Frank leaps of memory that I'm learning about.

"Big O liked to have this guy drive for him, like as a chauffeur, and this was a Puerto Rican guy who drank more than anyone I ever knew. Good choice for a driver, am I right? This guy would get all dressed up like a livery service driver, but no matter how professional he looked, he was always at least half in the bag, and one night he's so fucking drunk that he couldn't talk. We had some women, so we put him in the trunk. To sleep it off. Well, Big O put the car in a garage of his, and the next morning workers at Big O's shop were scared to open the trunk because they didn't know who the fuck was in there! So they had to call Big O to say, 'Hey man, you leave behind any kidnapped people or something?' And Big O came down to his shop hungover as shit and opens the trunk with an Uzi ready because he didn't remember it's his fucking chauffeur. And the chauffeur crawled out, straightened his tie, and just apologized because he didn't remember

— Rockstars and Executions —

how he got in the trunk.

"Michael Jackson was one of the few big shows I did in Miami. I've done Prince, Michael Jackson, and Bruce Springsteen there. The venue was the NFL stadium—it was called the Orange Bowl. That was one show Prince did where the whole cast or maybe just the two main guys from *Miami Vice* the show was there on the stage with Prince. They were dancing with him. That was the night I met Don Johnson and his partner on the show (Philip Seymour Thomas), and I was kinda laughing because I knew they were pissing off some real people with their stupid fucking pretend show. And man, they were kings then. They were all at Forge restaurant after the show with a smaller group, and I was there waiting for Prince, and yeah, the guys from *Miami Vice* were just as big as Michael Jackson and Prince. It was kinda wild. I remember that night the wine guy, the sommelier, said something funny that night. He said Miami restaurants are probably the only restaurants in the world where the busboys drive Rolls-Royces. I mean, there was a lot of coked-up money in Miami in those days, and the cars and the cash just filtered down. You know what's funny? Some Colombians and Cubans can eat a lot on cocaine—what the fuck is the deal with that? I could never eat anything after doing some toots. Honestly, I did not like Michael Jackson."

Ever seen the movie *Almost Famous*? Great film, about rock n roll, and most of the band-aids or groupie girls are like sixteen, max. Were there any bands or people who stand out in your memory as liking underage girls?

"Yeah, basically all the British acts—all of 'em. Rick James deserves another mention. I guess Michael Jackson too, but who the fuck knows? I didn't see anything goofy backstage. I did security once for him when he was still (with the) Jackson Five, and he was always more a private guy than a creep."

What was the attitude of security towards underage girls being around the bands?

"Who fucking cares? Definitely not the bands."

Well, that sucks.

"Elton John and Billy Joel were great acts. They toured together in 1994. They were touring, and so I met them in Virginia. I was asked to meet them at a show. It was drug-related. I did their shows in Virginia Beach, Richmond, and Greensboro. Back then, I had to be real careful about what I was doing because that early '90s era was very shaky for me. I was not in a good place. It had something to do with Bill Snouffer. Elton and Billy performed their own songs, and they performed each other's songs; it was a blast. Then Billy Joel started complaining a lot about Elton John. There was just a lot going on because Bill Snouffer was just being indicted for the things I was doing. So it was dicey, let's say. That tour was a big fucking deal though. They were both piano men, and they were good. They just didn't like each other after a while. They did a couple global tours first. Billy Joel made a big deal about not doing the tour again because he had some problems with Elton, or maybe he just had problems.

"Bruce Springsteen was a three-hour guy. He could go for three fucking hours, which in the rock and roll business is about the highest compliment there is. I mean, that's a lot of fucking energy. That's a lot of wear and tear. That's a lot of putting yourself out there. It's not easy.

"Actually, the albinos were some of the greatest musicians I've ever seen. Johnny Winter and his brother Edgar. Edgar played the sax. Johnny Winters died in Switzerland. For some reason, they were always easier on the heroin there, and so Johnny was there doing a tour, sure, but he knew Switzerland was where he could get good heroin.

"Bill Snouffer was pretty tight friends with Stevie Ray Vaughan. That was bad when he got killed in a helicopter crash. He was a fucking excellent guitarist and an even better showman. He had a little drug problem too—but a great fucking guy. He was on his way to the very top of the business and then disaster happened. That's around the time that Bill Snouffer fell into the ditch that killed him. He started doing every drug he could get his hands on. Bill Snouffer probably thought he was manning up by acting tough, like it didn't hurt him. But by manning up, he was fucking up. He was a mess. He was upset about Stevie Ray Vaughn dying, and so he basically started killing himself with drugs. It was a mess. Bill wouldn't listen to anybody that the shit was out of control.

"I think I told you how I stopped doing drugs? Well, I was living with [redacted] in Miami, and I had a couple Porsches, and I was kind of a loner. It was the end of the drugs. I was working out at night, then when I was done with working out, I would do some drugs and have some drinks. It was a weird time because I was thinking, 'Well, maybe I go all the way in.' It was a difficult time because the old deals were falling apart as more and more people went to jail and died, and I was thinking it might be the time to just go, to put it on the line and make new connections and be the biggest drug dealer I could. So I was there after working out, and I was breaking up a couple lines, and I don't think what happened next was a hallucination—it felt real to me, let's just say. Well, my father appeared to me, and he looked thirty years younger than when he did when he was dead. I was about to sniff a little cocaine and just have another crazy routine night and day, and my father appeared before me, and he said, 'Frankie, you need to quit the drugs right now.' I can't remember what happened next. I might've been crying for a little while, but that's the last time I was that fucked-up. I shouldn't have, but I did drugs after that. I straightened up a little bit, but I had to get hit by a couple more bad bumps in the road before I was finally scared enough to actually stop for good. But none of that would've happened if my Dad hadn't come back for me."

Frank shows me a video of Elton John and Billy Joel greeting each other on stage in front of a packed arena, the whole stage done up like a piano. Elton and Billy hug each other, wave to the crowd, and sit at two of the biggest pianos I've ever seen. In between the pianos, there, a little piece of Rock and Roll history, is Frank Sumner. In the video, he's wearing jeans, a tight black shirt, and dark sunglasses. The crowd roars and Frank's head tilts backwards, up, up, up to the heavens.

Frank and I went to lunch, celebrating the last day of interviews. Once it's clear Frank wants to keep talking, I excuse myself to the waitress and run to get my backpack with the laptop inside.

"Robert James was my younger brother, and he died at thirteen. His hair was blonder than mine and he had green eyes; he was left handed; he could ride horses bareback; and he was a badddddd student. He didn't even want to go to school anymore; he wanted to be in the trucking business full-time, and he was thirteen years old. Robert wasn't like my other brothers. He was a mix of my father and Uncle Stanley. He was different. No matter what happened he would've been different.

"I was gonna call my son and ask him, 'cause I never did, 'When did you know and how did you know your dad was in a bad business?' I never asked him that.

"I just know nobody fucked with him.

— Rockstars and Executions —

"I've only done two things in rock and roll as a fan. I went and saw James Brown, and I went and saw Stevie Wonder. Most of life was work. That was fun. I'm a loner, I like to move, and I'm comfortable here now with Kitty. But the summers are rough; they're crowded. You'd think I'd be okay being around crowds after years standing in front of thousands who were losing their minds, but nope, I never really noticed the crowds back then. I was busy being a drug dealer.

"Hey, you know you've brought Kitty's brain back, you know that? She was little more than comatose when I started training with her. I've got her walking now. She's arguing with me every day that she can go for more walks, further, longer. Now I've got her climbing the stairs instead of taking the elevator. When you started asking her questions—it's such a karmic thing—like, she said she hadn't thought about running cross-country in high school since she was in school, and it was the little things like remembering being a cross-country running star in high school for her to remember what it's like to be alive. She's alive again. And I'm going to figure out what makes her tick, what can push her to unlock the other parts of herself. She might not have known it since the strokes, but she's a fucking great person, man. She just lost sight of that.

"I'm a guy who doesn't want to see her hurt, in part because I've seen her do so much work to get where she is. When I got here, Kitty was basically comatose. If she ate anything, she would eat a bite of chocolate cake for breakfast. Think about that. She was drinking some sugar drink—I forget the name of that shit. She was eating or drinking the cheapest worst shit. I rolled with her, I got her exercising. I've got videos when I first met her, and I'm teaching her the breathing techniques. That's when it started, the feeling I have now. Having her be in the sun has made the most difference in her comeback. The sun is the most important thing. I've got her free walking this week, did I tell you that? She is free walking to the end of the dead end and back. She's doing that, and she's doing that without any pain medication. I don't want her on any medications, ever. And there's another party in her life. He wears a white coat, and he's a doctor. We're supposed to trust him, and all he wants is to dope her up with medication.

"Today is the biggest day of her life, and you know why? Today is the biggest day of her life because it's another day where she is herself."

I try to split the lunch bill. Frank waves me off, and I have to laugh when comparing our wallets. I have the wallet of a taxpayer: grocery store membership cards nestled between insurance cards and credit cards, a license, some paltry bills, the leather fading and crinkled.

Frank's wallet is a rubber band and a fat roll of crisp hundred-dollar bills.

Frank invites me to join him on a trip to Miami next month to meet some guys who he knows through Gilbert. Frank says to keep my phone on, maybe he'll call me from Colombia. Then he winks, and he says, "I'll let you know when Kitty finally swims in the ocean again."

Old habits die hard. I part company with Frank at the place he and Kathleen Behan share. Leaving their cul-de-sac, I pass windows that are still shuttered, closed against storms that may or may not appear. Behind me Frank turns, points up to the sky, and rocks as he begins doing a breathing exercise.

And that's that.

— Andrew Mallin —

About the Author

Andrew Mallin was born in Bridgeport, Connecticut in 1982 and never managed to dunk a basketball. Educated at the University of Connecticut and Hunter College, he has worked as a Geographer in New York, Boston, Washington and Munich. He now lives in Farmington, CT.

Rockstars and Executions is his first book.

Made in the USA
Columbia, SC
18 April 2025